HASTY PUDDING
and
KETTLE BROTH

Extracts from the diaries of
Bill Francis
of Minsterley

Edited by Peter Francis

Printed by Redverse Ltd
Unit F6, Greenwood Industrial Estate, Cartmel Drive
Shrewsbury SY1 3TB for PJ and JR Francis

ISBN No: 0 9519425 0 6

British Library Cataloguing-in-Publication Data.
A catalogue record for this book is available from the British Library

INTRODUCTION

My Grandfather, William (Bill) Francis, first saw the light of day on May 10th 1896. He was the fourth of five children born to William and Clara Francis of the Rock Farm. The farm clings precariously to the southern end of the Stiperstones and had been farmed since the 1780s by four generations of the Francis family. The land was at best rocky and shallow and many of my forebears also worked at the nearby lead mines to supplement their farming activities.

Having left school at the age of twelve, my Grandfather worked in various "no-end jobs" until 1914 when he joined the King's Shropshire Light Infantry as a signaller. During the four years of the First World War he experienced the full horrors of the battlefields of northern Europe. Later, in the 1920s, he worked underground at the Bog mine on the Stiperstones, but spent most of his working life as a bricklayer and jobbing builder. After returning home from the War and marrying, he lived at Appletree Farm, The Grit; Lake Cottage, Asterley and, in his later years, Station Terrace, Minsterley — always within sight (and cycling distance) of his beloved Stiperstones. His wife of 57 years, Adeline ("surely the best ever") died in 1979. Not long after, he decided to keep a record "trivial or otherwise, of daily events which affect my person."

He kept this diary faithfully until his death in 1989, just before his 93rd birthday. It is a lyrical and often humorous account of day to day activities, vivid memories and a unique and forthright philosophy of life. His love of the natural world, his strong sense of fellowship for his friends and neighbours, his openness and honesty and, above all, his hatred of injustice are all interwoven in a rich tapestry of words and ideas.

Editing his diaries and preparing them for publication has taken three long years. I must thank my family for their patience and help during that time and particularly my daughters Heather aged 9 and Angela 11 (Bill's great grandchildren) for the drawings which help illustrate these pages.

All profits from the sale of this book will be shared equally between Oxfam and Amnestry International, two of the charities actively supported by my Grandfather.

Peter Francis
1992

No 4, Station Terrace fronted by the 'old shop'

I, William W Francis, by the mercy of the Eternal being at this time eighty six years, seven months and twenty one days of age and by that same mercy having a sound mind, a healthy body, a free will and an independent spirit, have decided from this day forward to keep a record, trivial or otherwise, of daily events which affect my person.

16 January 1983

Fine morning. 50 degrees in shop. Usual chores. Afternoon visit with J&S, P&J via Bishop's Castle and Clun to Hopton Castle where ancestor, one Richard Francis (reputedly Colour Sergeant or Standard Bearer), formed part of small defence force under member of More family. They defended castle for Cromwell against Royalists. All except More had throats cut on surrender. Moral — better die fighting than be killed like a pig. Small square ruins, but remains of moat etc interesting. Took three photos although light poor. Back via Lydbury North. Watched "Mastermind" 8.40-9.10.

1 March 1983

Arose early. Bright morn at first. 50 degrees in shop, weather mild. Cycled Westbury in afternoon. Took some chrysanth cuttings. Bridge Hotel for drink 9.30pm. Back home to hear "One Thousand Welsh Voices" which lasted twenty minutes. Near perfect. Hope for plenty of Welsh singers in Kingdom of Heaven, if I ever reach it. Slight rain tonight.

10 March 1983

Arose early. Mild morn, 52 degrees in shop. Felt lazy so decided to have easy day. Went down village to purchase pork chop for dinner and local postcard to send to C&F. Met PA who gave me 50p, said he owed it me from two years ago. Had forgotten. Replied "Thanks, that means a bottle of beer". It reminded me of an old boy I knew years ago. He was fond of his pipe, a drop of ale and a bob or two sometimes on the horses. One day the Vicar called on him, urged him to repent and give up the world. "No need to" replied the old boy "the world gave me up years ago". ED called. Brought book about Cornish tin mines. Sorted out freezer food-containers in afternoon and cleaned them. Finished day easy.

2 May 1983

Still raining after 48 hours. Visibility poor. 58 degrees in shop. Suppose this is real May Day as 1st was a Sunday. Must have been a better climate when AE Housman wrote his "Ludlow Fair" or Tennyson his "May Queen". If little Alice were to be May Queen this year she would need a nylon coat and hood. Also, no trees clothed in green or emerald meadows — and "Ludlow Fair" not to mention Clun, Bishops Castle and Craven Arms would be one big puddle. Having lived through those days myself, can say that in spite of the abject poverty of most country people, they lived closer to nature and their God. On a fine sunny morning a spontaneous joy would well up in their hearts, even if it was only short lived. As ever I suppose, the old long for the past and the young for the future. Both suffer from self-deception. There can be no perfection till Shiloh comes. Even so, come. Did weekly wash — small one. Made seed boxes for self and girls next door. ED called for natter. Settling down now for TV and books.

21 May 1983

Mild again. 60 degrees in shop. Rain forecast for afternoon, which materialised. Attended J Parry's funeral service at Methodist Church, 12 noon. Cannot understand why funeral services are such mournful occasions. If — as most Christians profess to believe — death either before or after the Resurrection is the gateway to a happier existence, they should be occasions, if not for joy, at least for deep thought. I do not expect in the ordinary way to die myself cf 1st Corinthians 15; 51/52 (Moffat translation). I have every hope of being alive when Shiloh comes. If however it is the will of the Eternal that it should be otherwise and my executors, ie my sons and daughter, decide to hold a religious service over my mortifying remains, they should make a cheerful theme of it with such songs as: 'All People that on Earth do Dwell' or 'Come Let us Join the Cheerful Throng' or at least 'Oh Lord of Heaven and Earth and Sea' or 'O God of Bethel'. I would also advocate a round of drinks at the local.

27 May 1983

Mild morn. 60 degrees in shop. Became cooler in evening. More work at Ashley's. Went down village to post letter and visit shop. FW called with Watchtower magazine. Had discussion. Philip called on cycle ride. Said was going to Lydham-Plowden-over Cwm Head-Marshbrook-Church Stretton and back home. Gave him cup of coffee and wished I was young enough to accompany him. On further thought, in that case could not be his Grandfather. Cycled to Westbury. Jim not at shop, but called for tea 6.30. Bed earlier tonight.

5 June 1983

Warmest morn yet. 65 degrees in shop and continued fine with sunshine until 6pm. Fed kitten next door and saw to greenhouse plants. After breakfast of cornflakes and milk, got out best cycle and dusted it. When for delightful short cycle ride — Pontesbury, Habberley and around the country lanes. Back over Callow. Fields and hedgerows delightful and full of colour. I loitered to enjoy it all. After a wet cold Spring, Summer at last — full of her glorious divinity — lay stretched before me. As I breathed the pure air, away from stinking cars, I felt I could at last drink deep of the cup that nature held out to me. The ordered disorder of nature is more beautiful and wonderful than the designs of man. Man in his infancy must have had a delightful time as he wandered about and left his waste behind him for nature to recycle. He fed his body from the earth he trod and accepted all things as a gift from God, till overcrowding caused him to acquire wealth and to drag his spirit in the mire.

And so to bed. Busy day tomorrow.

22 July 1983

Weather warm. 75 degrees in shop. Finished building new boundary wall. Should be trouble-free from now onwards. Good job done, but not altogether pleased with the quality of my work. Perhaps slipping through old age. Cycled to Westbury. Cool breeze. Jim did not call for tea tonight so had solitary one. Still picking raspberries. They appear to be like the cruise of oil and meal belonging to the widow who the prophet Elijah stayed with during the famine in Israel. I have no complaints, rather give thanks to the Eternal for the beautiful fruits of the good earth. Weather thundery tonight. Likely rain before morning. Looking back on what I have just written, it occurs to me that the prophet and the widow and her son would have had a very restricted diet if the record as related in the Book of Kings is correct. It states that no dew or rain fell on Israel for three years. Small wonder the boy was sick unto death. Some of my raspberries would have supplied the much needed vitamins.

7 August 1983
Sunday. Very warm, 75 degrees in shop. Wrote letter to Pat. Found some net curtains which Adeline had put away in a drawer and fixed them in back porch. Started to church 5.20. When I reached the church gate a family was unloading for what I supposed was a baptism. As I do not believe in baptism of infants — they should be allowed to reach maturity and be baptised of their own free will — I passed on. In my childhood days a babe who died before baptism was not allowed to be buried in consecrated ground. As if a loving Father and Creator of all mankind would discriminate against a helpless child because some tupenny ha'penny CofE parson had not sprinkled a few drops of water on it. CofE much improved since then, but still has pockets of bigotry and religious dogma. But still, JC stated emphatically "Let them all grow together until the Harvest". As I am convinced the Harvest is very near, who am I to decide otherwise? So I returned home. Listened to 6pm News then went for delightful cycle ride — Pontesbury, New Mills Lane, Hinton, Lea Cross, Nox, Yockleton, Westbury and back home. An easy jog of 1½ hours. Took photo of railway at Yockleton and of Pink Elephant pub sign. Was quite fresh and not at all fatigued on return.

21 August 1983
Warm. 75 degrees in shop. Warm and showers later. Household chores. Plucked eight corn cobs. Put six in freezer. Took two for J&S at dinnertime. Rested and nap in afternoon. Later decided go for walk. Put on new pair of rather heavy walking shoes. These made feet and legs ache, so returned after one hour very tired and very hungry. Made thick sandwich of ham, cheese and tomato. Slice of fruit pie and pot of pure Indian tea. Enjoyed excellent meal while listening to Beethoven's ninth symphony on BBC 2 from Edinburgh Festival. If — as is often stated — "music is the food of love", it is also food and solace for the lonely soul. When the Eternal evicted the human race from Paradise, the two greatest comforts He allowed us were music and Scotch Whiskey. They can be enjoyed simultaneously and enhance each other. When the Kingdom of Heaven comes to earth (I am not saying 'if') I am sure these two will be available for man's enjoyment. JC told His followers that He would drink new wine with them in His Father's Kingdom. To the best of my knowledge, whiskey was not available at the period of history. If it was, the Scots kept it to themselves.

11 September 1983
Cold, wet morn. 58 degrees in shop. Household chores including cleaning bedroom and changing sheets. Rest of day — reading and contemplation. Church 5.30-6.30. But life is not all seriousness. Some lighter moments. For instance, in advice column of today's paper: Dear Miss M-"What is the minimum requirement of a bride setting up a new home?" Miss M- "A bridegroom". And again, for some reason called to mind a conversation heard between two ladies during last war about difficulty of furnishing new home during rationing (we all had clothing coupons). One lady remarked "But our Nora will be alright, she works in a laundry". Such is life. Old time Music Hall again on TV tonight.

26 September 1983

Back home after weekend in Bicton. House empty and cold. 58 degrees in shop. Felt desolated and lonely for short period. Soon recovered. Sun dispersed fog and house warmed with fire in Parkray. No hot water so delayed weekly wash until tomorrow.

Afternoon. Water heated up quicker than expected so did weekly wash. One article (a bed sheet) badly torn so had to put it on clothes line in position that tear did not show. Must preserve dignity. Hope to get two more turns from it (quiet laugh). Day became fine and warm.

2 October 1983

Fine sunny morn. 62 degrees in shop. Housework, then attended to flowers. Book and idleness until dinnertime. Miss D brought me a pie. There is a sadness which grows from the seeds of remembered times and a weariness which springs unasked for from the remembered fountains of youth. A yearning for times past and places and people long gone, tucked away into the infinite mists of the past. Such a time happened this evening when I attended with John a Harvest Festival at the delightful little CofE church at Snailbeach. In my childhood days seventy, eighty, ninety years ago when people lived closer to nature and their God and every small church of any denomination held its Harvest Festival, the whole community for miles around would attend them all. They would fill the places to overflowing and sing, with spontaneous and joyful exultation, praises to the Eternal for gifts real or imagined. By present day conditions, gifts then were small and poverty was rife. A boy who had two suits of clothes and two pairs of boots was the envy of the others. We polished our weekday boots with penny tins of old fashioned blacking for Sunday service. If that ran out we had to make do with the black lead which mother used to polish the grate. Well, times have altered and some churches do not now hold these Festivals. I heard of one CofE minister who described them as "The Feast of the Pumpkin". However the one at Snailbeach was a joyous occasion in spite of a few vacant seats. May it continue to prosper.

9 October 1983

Cool and damp. 60 degrees in shop. Household chores, little else. Attended to chrysanths in greenhouse. Some showing colour. Rather early, perhaps because of dull days. Must purchase some later-flowering ones next season. I like to have a few blooms for Christmas and New Year. Dinner J&S. Church 5.30-6.30. Only seven in congregation. Minister must find it a bit of a bind talking to so few when he could be at home with his family. A light drizzle, so could not take a walk afterwards. Wrote letter to Pat. Watched first part of film "Gone with the Wind" on BBC1. Spectacular no doubt, but then war is spectacular looked at from the outside and the American Civil War was only a damp squib compared with today's conflicts. I remember during 1914-18 War five mines being exploded under German lines. Spectacular indeed to me, watching from half a mile away. How many German fathers, sons, husbands, lovers were blown towards Heaven before descending to Hell, I do not know. Dresden burning would have been spectacular viewed from the air when that beautiful city was destroyed by our bombers during Second World War. The Atomic Bomb bursting over Hiroshima would be spectacular from the plane that dropped it. But how many broken bodies and minds are there still alive in this world today caused by these things — and still worse to come? There but for the mercy and grace of the Eternal could be I.

10 October 1983

Cool, 60 degrees in shop. Arose rather late. Household chores and weekly wash. Quarterly membership magazine from Amnesty International in post. Also leaflet with smashing young blonde lady extolling the use of Persil. Wrote serio-comic letter to Lever Brothers asking why they gave the impression that only young blonde housewives used their product, pointing out that old gentlemen and ladies also use it for their laundry work. Look forward with some amusement to a reply. Made pancakes for tea.

10 November 1983

Mild but dull. 58 degrees in shop. Visited Shrewsbury on early bus for sundry purchases and business. Bought a pair of trousers. No buttons as usual, so had to sew set on myself tonight. Jim phoned. Not at Westbury tomorrow. Advert in gardening magazine "Do not let your garden kill you. We will do it for you". Take it as you like, but my definition and thought would be — much better to drop off whilst working in the garden than die in bed. If I were a member of the Synod of the CofE (which God forbid) I would introduce a motion adding two phrases to the Litany: "From self pity, good Lord deliver us" and "From dying in bed, good Lord deliver us". But, as JC said, He did not come to call the self-righteous, but sinners to repentance. So will be unlikely to take much notice of me or the CofE.

13 November 1983

Rather cold. 55 degrees in shop with cold east wind. So-called Armistice Sunday when ministers of religion, politicians and the establishment perpetuate that old lie of the glorious dead of two World Wars who died for freedom. Balls! If they had seen how the poor buggers died — bodies torn to shreds and still alive, boys 18-19 with legs blown off moaning "Mother, oh mother" as their blood gushed out — they would think it anything but glorious. I am reminded of a verse by the poetess Katharine Tynan "There they go marching all in step so gay! Smooth-cheeked and golden, food for shells and guns. Blithely they go as to a wedding day, the mother's sons". And all the freedom those who came back earned was the freedom to live in poverty while the rich manufacturers of weapons of destruction schemed where they could start the next war.

But on a lighter note, took a five mile walk this afternoon. Met one other hardy soul, an oldish lady also out walking. When I reached Plox Green, was greeted by another lady who gave me two toffees to sustain me until I reached home. I told her I would "dance at her wedding". I often say that. Will now eat the second toffee.

Off to war, 1914

6 December 1983

Cold morning. 45 degrees in shop. Weekly wash and household chores. Dark dismal day. Settled in by fire 4pm. RL phoned. Bad cold. No pub or dominoes tonight. Welcomed this. Not too good myself. Item on News of death of Bishop of Woolwich who wrote the book "Honest to God" to take, he said, the myth out of Christianity. I see no myth. JC lived, was murdered by His own people (as foretold by prophets hundreds of years before) and was resurrected by the Eternal (as also foretold). Afterwards He walked, talked even ate with many of His followers. If this were not true they would have just dispersed thinking they had been deceived. So sure were they, that many gladly died a violent death for the sake of their belief. Where the myth? And to the gospel they preached — that JC died and rose again to save mankind from its sins — I would also add, to save the bulk of mankind from the sins of society. The innocent man in a prison cell, put there by laws made to keep the rich in power and enforced by a politically motivated judiciary and a corrupt police force; the starving Third World nations suffering from the exploitation of the rich ones. If I asked for or collected money for the poor I should be called a Christian gentleman. If I shouted out for their just rights, I should be called a 'bloody Commie'. My dream, the one for which JC said He came, is the fulfillment of the words of the prophet Isaiah: 'Set at liberty the captive. Let the oppressed go free. Break down every yoke'. To share one's food with the hungry and provide shelter and clothing for the homeless and the poor. I realize that most of this cannot happen until JC returns to take charge. There are many signs that time is just around the corner. Even so come.

5 February 1984

Colder. 45 degrees in shop. Strong cold winds outside. Household chores before dinner with J&S. ED called for half hour. Took walk up Leigh Road later. Only pedestrian met — one foxhound, apparently young, by Rea Brook Farm. It followed me for some time before I told it to "get". It got. Back home listened to "Down You Way" with Brian Johnston from Wellingborough. Two interesting items. One, an importer of grain and fruit, said his company was first to wash and prepack dried fruit. Before that, he said, raisins etc contained a quantity of goat droppings because goats wandered among the fruit as it dried in the open. As all dried fruit was sold loose when I was young, I must have consumed quite a lot of goat droppings. Could be. Next one, an old cavalry man who had been through First World War, said last time used as cavalry was at Battle of Arras in April 1917. Said they lost half their horses taking Monchy Le Preux. Well I was in that battle as a signaller with 8th Infantry Brigade and we had cleared the enemy from the village before they came along. Most of their horses were lost to barbed wire, machine gun and artillery fire. A pitiable sight. In spite of the usual tragedies and comrades killed, I have several interesting and humorous memories of that battle. Continual rain and wind outside tonight.

12 February 1984

Mild morn. 55 degrees in shop, but wind shifted to east and became colder during day. Did little during morning but change bed sheets and tidy up generally. Had planned cycle ride for late afternoon, but as wind cold decided on walk instead. Met several others with same idea, and enjoyable it was. Birds singing, fields green and many snowdrops out by habitations. Arrived back home 5pm, after 4½-5 miles, untired and full of self confidence — could have gone round again, or so I thought. Instead, lit front room fire and made pot of pure Indian tea. Delicious! Win then phoned: "Coming out for stuff from freezer and eggs forgotten last Thursday." If weather continues fair must arise earlier in future. I am apt to repeat myself on this subject and, with that in mind, remember people from the long distant past with the same habit. For instance, during my sojourn in the British Army during and after the First World War 1914-1920, we had a man in our company (later Sgt Bond) who always believed in anything "to a certain extent". Everything was "to a certain extent". People would ask his opinion just to hear him say it. Then there was the dear old Rector of our parish 'The More' when I was a child (if I ever was one) Rev Ridley Retton who in conversation kept on repeating "exactly, exactly" or rather it sounded to me like "eggactly". He was a dear old man, meek and sympathetic to all. If, as JC said, the meek do "inherit the earth" in due time, I for one would agree that RR should be entitled to a rather larger share than most of us. Not that I am meek myself. In fact I am often aggressive when confronted with hypocrisy or injustice. So was JC, in spite of the things written in children's story books. Calm and frosty outside tonight. Have switched radiator on in shop.

7 March 1984

Mild. 58 degrees in shop. Mild all day but cloudy and dull. Cycled to Westbury in afternoon. Saw 'Timewatch' on TV last night. Old professor said he had come to the conclusion that all men were fools. Nothing remarkable there. I had reached the same conclusion by the time I was eighteen years old, also that I myself was one of the worst specimens. It has been said that humans are superior to animals in that they are able to reason. A more vulgar definition says they drink when they are not thirsty and have sex all the year round. That does not concern us here. Even when people do reason, they do it from their own point of view, thinking that other persons will have the same outlook. Only a minute number of people can empty themselves and see events through the eyes and mind of another. Perhaps one of the most outstanding examples of this was Field Marshal Montgomery. He placed himself in Rommel's position and so conquered. Mild with very low clouds this evening. Became dark early.

11 March 1984

Rather cool, 48 degrees. Usual household chores. After dinner went with J&S and S's mother to More where my sister is to be buried next Tuesday. Journey back via Snead, Churchstoke, Montgomery, Chirbury and Marton. By this time, rain was falling and weather cold. Stayed indoors after.

A curious thing happened to me last night. Sometime during the hours of darkness I suddenly awoke and a voice from inside me or outside said "You wrote in your diary the other day that all men were fools and you yourself were one of the worst specimens. Have you considered the alternative?" I sat up in bed and thought for a short time. If all were wise, never made a wrong decision or a mistake, what would life be like? No jokes, no fun made of each other or oneself. No pieces to pick up and put right. I decided, on the whole better a world populated by fools than wise men and slept again in peace.

25 March 1984

Quarter Day, Lady Day and first day of Summer time. 50 degrees in shop. Cold and dry outside but rain and strong winds later. Looked like another "Sunday at home". Have a volume upstairs somewhere, came from Ad's people I believe, one year's bound copy of the weekly periodical "Sunday at Home". Shall have to get it out if we have many more weekends like the present. During my childhood in the last part of the nineteenth century and the early part of the twentieth, Sunday was vastly different from today. The Sabbath was so strictly kept that people would allow their farm crops to be destroyed rather than gather them on a Sunday. The only paper allowed for reading in my home was the "Christian Herald". It was a terrible weekly with anecdotes outside the bounds of either fact or fiction and a couple of sermons, one by Rev T de Wit Talmage an American who at the early age of eight or nine I thought to be an eloquent hypocrite and one by CH Spurgeon who I looked upon as a genuine Christian character. So much for childhood insight. "Out of the mouthes of babes and sucklings comes forth wisdom". Regarding the Sabbath, I am at one with JC who said "The Sabbath was made for man, not man for the Sabbath". He meant, I suppose, that it was good for mankind to have one day's idleness in seven to rest and rehabilitate the body and that if anyone was too much of a BF to take advantage of such a blessing that was his own concern. We, on the other hand, were taught that the Sabbath was invented so that an Almighty God could have a stick to beat us with. As regards the fourth Jewish commandment, its true purpose would be to prevent slaves and servants being exploited by their masters, trade unions not being invented then. About 6pm got fed up with being indoors so put a mac on and went for a walk in the rain. Only people I met were a motorist who asked in a cultured voice if I could direct him to the Village Hall and three young people on ponies who waved a cheerful greeting, which I returned. After a sharp walk — still raining — I reached home just in time to see "Highway" on ITV from St. David's, S Wales.

11 June 1984

Warm morn. 65 degrees in shop and fine day forecast. Decided to have day out with cycle among those most delightful hills of Shropshire, the Stiperstones. So, equipped with flask, sandwiches, camera and a good book, got self and cycle placed on a Valley bus as far as Hemford. Disembarked there and travelled through Shelve, Pennerley and The Bog. Spent a few minutes at Shelve Top surveying the beauty of the countryside, of which one could never have a surfeit. At Pennerley called on an old acquaintance who lives in a delightful stone cottage by himself, having never experienced the joys of matrimony. From there to The Bog and The Rock. Settled near an old cottage (now a wreck) and for two and a half hours enjoyed the peace and solitude which only true lovers of the countryside seek and enjoy. It was broken only by a party of about thirty school-children and three teachers who had also been exploring the rocks. I visited the well which had once served the cottage (I have named it "The Well of Salvation" because of the rough stony path one must tread to reach it). After pouring out an oblation to the Eternal for all the loving kindness and beauty of nature so lavishly bestowed on the human race, I took a long deep drink of its pure, ice-cold waters. Returning to my cycle, I made my way via Rhadley, The Nynd and The Runnis to the Shrewsbury-Bishop's Castle road and so home. A day to be remembered, perhaps more so because of the increasing infirmities of age which must eventually overtake me. But for the present, all is well.

"Lyric to the Stiperstones" by one of its sons

One morn I took my cycle to the hills;
The sun was shining and the world was gay
And solitude and peace which ever fills
The heart of those who seek a peaceful day.

The scent of hawthorn blossom filled the air,
Rowan, laburnum made a joyful scene;
Gorse, broom and other bushes flourish there,
Enrich the senses, make the mind serene.

Come back the time as at this world's creation
When all the morning stars together sang
And all the sons of God in high elation
Shouted for joy until the heavens rang.

Though small the things that swell my happy song
That to the poorest of our race belong,
My heart is filled with joyful notes of praise
For all the blessings of the passing days.

Oh sweet the evening dews and May time showers
That raise beauty from its Winter bowers,
Bring back the green of earth and the blue skies —
Uplift the heart, give pleasure to mine eyes.

For the hills are in the soul of me,
A devil is in my heels,
I am tired of rows of houses
And the roar of lorry wheels;
I hunger for the mountains
Where the rivers have their source
And the winds of all creation
Are free to blow their course.

Here trembling dew on early blossoms rests
Or shines like silver on the spider's nest
And here a boundless heath before me lies,
Warmed by the sun and watered from the skies.

I wonder as a I contemplate the view,
Was old Amphion here when time was new
To play his hornpipes here with joyful zest,
Bring to these mountains all of nature's best?

Here generous nature sheds her bounties free,
Food for all birds and pollen for the bee;
Here nests the hawk where mankind seldom trod
And roving foxes seek their meat from God.

Far are we here from men who with selfish greed
Value their wealth above their neighbour's need
And politicians who with piouz zeal
Seek their own power before their country's weal.

Here are these hillsides clad with native thorn
And rocky outcrops formed e'er man was born;
Here nature's sculptures formed of naked stone
And one is aptly named as 'Satan's Throne'.

In times long past stood many a lowly cott
Where happy miners tilled their tiny plot;
All that remains — a crumbling heap of stones
And creeping nature claims again its own.

And here the school where in my childhood days
We did our songs and sang our hymns of praise.
Change and decay now round its precincts lie,
As like myself it waits its turn to die.

As lengthened shadows mark the close of day,
I cycle slowly on my homeward way;
Thankful for modern roads and, come the night,
One of those boons to man — electric light.

WF

1 July 1984

Sunday. Slightly warmer. 62 degrees in shop. Very warm during day. Head cold seems to have passed but stomach still queasy, so went easy on food. Reading in Summer House, house work and odd jobs during morning. Dinner J&S. Reading, "Gardener's Question Time" and "Down Your Way" on radio until tea. Enjoyed good meal — bread and butter with Win's strawberry jam and slice of fruit cake. 6.30 took walk up Callow Road as far as Bank Farm. Hedges glorious with honeysuckle and wild roses. Picked bunch of honeysuckle for kitchen table. Perfume delightful and always further enhanced by humid atmosphere such as in late evening or early dewey morn. How many times I wonder, during my long and varied life white cycling to work in early morn, have I been bodily delighted and spiritually uplifted by the sight and smell of it in the hedgerows. I wonder if there was honeysuckle in the Garden of Eden. Every time I study the story of the Creation, I get the impression that Adam must have been an extremely weak character. Had I been in his place I would have said to God "Do not blame my wife, it was I who picked the fruit". It is unlikely that I should have been believed however because of the universal fact that all men are liars, especially where women are concerned. I will now get a can of beer.

22 July 1984

Warm. 70 degrees in shop. Slight mist. Very warm later. Heard on radio, man in USA who advocated jogging as way to good health had died himself from heart attack when jogging. Opinion — would say that good health is brought about by sensible living. If someone insults and poisons their body during the first half of their life, it is hardly feasible to believe that they can retrieve their youth and vigour when turned forty, by jogging. Cycle ride in afternoon. Only two more cyclists out. Very warm. Rested few minutes by Yockleton railway bridge. Old lady down road expecting visit from relatives, had washed large counterpane — thinking they would help her wring it and get it on clothes line. They did not arrive. So in dire extremity came to me for assistance. Duly obliged. Such is life.

5 September 1984

Cooler. 60 degrees in shop and cool all day. Visited Shrewsbury again to collect Travel Tokens and buy supplies, mostly for stock. With cooler weather after a very warm spell, one's body needs a bigger and better diet. Cool outside tonight, but have a fire so house is warm inside. Yarn on radio this morning too good to be passed up. A lady relating how her husband proposed to her (well I presume she was a lady as she had that title, but my experience in a long life is that they are more often to be found among the so-called lower orders than the upper. Definition "Lady" Collin's National Dictionary: "A gentle and noble woman. A kind woman of refined manners"). But to resume. This woman said that although she was in love with her man, she did not wish to accept too quickly. However, when she noticed he had tears in his eyes she did and said "yes", only to discover later that he had been sitting on a thorny cactus, hence the tears. When I proposed to my wife I had a broken arm in a sling. She said "I won't promise", but did so later. Must have been pity. I know of no other reason. Stayed up late watching Benjamin Britten's opera "Gloriana". Sarah Walker not a very convincing Queen, but costumes marvellous. It was supposed to be an immoral age, but a chap must have had one hell of a job seducing his girl friend with all those clothes. But as always, where there is a will there is a way. Oh dear, written a lot tonight.

9 September 1984

As yesterday. 65 degrees in shop. Arose rather late at 9.15. More or less idle morning after household chores. ED called for talk. Short nap after dinner. Decided to take long walk, but after about one mile got caught in heavy storm so returned home. Was very wet from knees down. After tea, listened "Highway" on ITV. Ken Dodd and Harry Secombe speaking about laughter. Said only humans laughed and that it was the greatest blessing ever bestowed by the Eternal on the human race. I heartily agree. They could have added that humans were the only animals that prayed, or had need to. However, I know of other pleasant sounds beside laughter. One would be the sound of good beer (paid for by someone else) splashing into a pint mug. "Highway" filmed in the Lake District and Keswick. Sang that haunting and moving melody "you tak the high road, and I'll tak the low". But of course the boy was wrong. They will meet again in a very near future, so sure am I of the eventual salvation of the human race. Calm and clear outside now. A near full moon rising in the eastern sky.

16 September 1984

Mild and calm. 65 degrees in shop. Household chores in morning. Dinner J&S one hour earlier as they were visiting Hereford in the afternoon. So decided to take long cycle ride. Encountered eleven other cyclists. One young couple — with children and car — gathering hazelnuts and another couple — with children, on foot — seeking blackberries. Exchanged greetings with them and passed on. On reaching Half Way House felt vigorous and fresh so decided continue to Bulthy and Breidden Hills (a favourite spot of mine). Duly arrived, but found had to walk up banks which I could ride once with ease. I had time to waste so was not unduly worried. At Bulthy there is a triangular piece of ground — now covered with trees — where once stood a cottage in which my mother as a child lived with her grandfather (1850s and 60s). He was a well-sinker and wooden-pump maker. Must have been a skilled trade. One had to bore a two inch hole straight through a six foot length or so of 9 x 9 or 12 x 12. There are still some around, but preserved as museum pieces. Took a photo of the site and then climbed partly up the Bulthy Hill, where my mother in her childhood must often have trod. Away from the world — a place of peace, quietness, serenity and isolation. The vista opened before one must be amongst the most striking and beautiful in England or Wales. To the west the hills and mountains of North and Central Wales, to the north Shrewsbury and the North Shropshire plain and to the east the Shropshire hills. One could feel like Moses viewing the Promised Land, except that Moses had not left his cycle at the foot of the hill. So I ceased romancing, collected bike and returned home via Vennington, Westbury, Asterley and Malehurst. Found Jim and Bob had come to visit me. Apologised and gave them tea and cakes. Later watched TV — programme about Scottish Isles. Finished on Iona. Reader read Isaiah 61. Oh dear it is midnight, I must to bed.

7 October 1984

Mild, cool wind at first. 60 degrees in shop. Idle morning after housework. ED called for natter. 3pm decided walk up Callow and seek few blackberries for tea. None on roadside so walked along old rail track and found ample in jungle near. Must relate here a yarn ED told me this morning. Too long to relate in detail, but in essence about a Plymouth

Rock cockerel he won at a whist drive when he and his wife lived at Snailbeach. The cockerel escaped and they found it in a tree at Lordshill. When dislodged it flew back home, hitting a cottage chimney on the way and causing almighty havoc to a Sunday dinner being cooked below. Well, every time I thought of it I started laughing. Had anyone seen me they would have sure thought I was a nutcase. On way home had a short talk with a lady who gave me two good eating apples. A little later, caught up with a short stoutish old man with an Irish accent. Held a brief conversation with him about trifles. He reminded me of an uncle I used to have. I met him only once, about 1905 when I was nine years of age, but clearly carry his image in my memory. A dear old man, waggoner on a farm at Cross Green, Berwick. A time and way of life long past. May the Eternal preserve his memory. One more to welcome or be welcomed by at the regeneration. After tea with the blackberries, watched "River Journey" down the Nile on BBC 2 — the longest river in the world from its source to Cairo — a picture of life on its banks in some cases unchanged since before Christ. Joy and despair, exultation and depression. Such I suppose, to a greater or lesser degree, is life for all of us. How many lanes must a man walk down till he finally comes to his end?

14 October 1984

Rather mild. 60 degrees in shop. Housework, including changing bed sheets. Then settled to read "Observer". ED called. Had a jovial hour's talk. After lunch got out cycle for medium length ride. Only thing of note — passed about 15 people of mixed ages at entrance to Worthen village. Either sponsored walk or organised hike. Back home, cooked plum and apple with custard for tea. This reminded me of Tommy Tickler's Plum and Apple Jam with which the lower ranks on the Western Front were deluged during the Great War and the song we sang about it (the Officer's Mess had the strawberry jam). It was reported that TT had two large farms in East Anglia where he grew the swedes and mangolds for the jam, with plum and apples planted on the perimeter for the flavour. Well, we laughed and we died. Three quarters of a million of my generation — and for what? Very mild tonight and dry outside.

4 November 1984

Cool and dry. 55 degrees in shop. Arose rather late. Had cup of tea and biscuit. Fetched "Observer" — price now gone up to 45p. Housework and attended flowers. ED called for long natter. 3pm decided on lengthy walk and this time did circuit without hindrance from rain, or other mishap. Met only one individual, a lady walking her dog in Drury Lane. Returned home refreshed and full of vigour. Listened "Down Your Way" from Gloucester. Finished remains of strawberries and cream from yesterday. Interesting subject on Channel Four tonight, 8.15 — midnight. The trial of Richard III. I have never harboured the thought that he was the deformed monster that Shakespeare's play portrays him to be. Contemporary history shows a rather different story. But then Shakespeare was writing a play not history. Anyway, Richard died in battle which cannot be said of any leader for the last few hundred years. They leave the common herd to do that and take the merit to themselves;

praise the "glorious dead" at yearly intervals and leave the maimed in body and mind to live and die in poverty and obscurity. 8.15 coming up now. Will pass opinion later.

An interesting 2¾ hours and the verdict of the jury was that Richard III was not guilty of his nephews' murder, with which verdict I entirely agree. It matters not, for he, like all of mankind, must in the last analysis stand before the throne of eternal justice from which there is no hiding place. Goodnight.

6 November 1984

Cold and wet. 50 degrees in shop and same all day. Arose late after a dream in which I had sold an old car and several other items to a dealer who tried to get away without paying. A fight occurred, at which point I awoke feeling rather depressed. Whether the depression was due to the fact that I had not finished the fight, or that I was so old that people tried to take advantage of me, I could not decide. No doubt Freud would have seen a sexual angle to it. But at 88? I ask you.

But here again it could be argued that the patriarch Abraham was 99 when he sired Isaac and, through him, the whole of the Jewish race. Ah, but Abraham lived in a warm and sunny climate. Had it been England and November, it would have been:

> No go for the Jewish race,
> No go as a sire,
> He'd have spent his time supping mutton broth
> And gathering wood for the fire.

But I have no doubt that the invisible power that controls the destiny of the human race and the entire universe causes such things to happen at the right place and the right time. So be it. Bought a few supplies down village. Wrote letter or two, including airmail to David and Pauline, Arizona, USA. Had kipper for tea.

25 November 1984

Cold, clear morning. 52 degrees in shop. Usual Sunday morn chores. ED called for talk. Dinner J&S. 2pm listened "Gardener's Question Time". Later took walk up Callow Hill for change. I suppose at some future time — say after next year's Summer — if and when cycling becomes a hardship and travail as I approach my ninetieth birthday, I shall have to depend more and more on walking instead. This presupposes of course that I shall still be walking this Earth. For all my past life is mine no more and the future is in the hands of the Eternal. I have only the present — and that unstable. "Time", writes the poet, "like an ever rolling stream". With age, the stream becomes a rushing roaring cataract strewn with the boulders of life's increasing hazards. By the mercy of the Eternal I have not struck any yet. But to return to my walk. After the heavy rains of recent weeks, the air was clear and cold, bracing and perhaps exhilarating. The hills stood out in sharp relief and on Aston Moors many acres under small lakes, such as I have not seen for many years. Very few other people about. Travelled perhaps a furlong beyond Bank Farm and returned home as sun was setting. Enjoyed nice cup of tea. Listened "Down Your Way" with Brian Johnston, also "Highway" with Harry Secombe. Both good programmes. "Royal Variety Show" on BBC 1 tonight. Listened some of it but thought it boring and wet. Could be me of course. Last part of show very very good.

15 December 1984

Bright and cold at first, cloudy later. 47 in shop. Usual household chores. Afternoon cleaned and tidied old shop. Hope to have very nice chrysanths for Christmas week. Was fearful one time they would all be finished. But now a few, especially Red Perfection and Snowshine, will be at their best. Must make a note to take extra cuttings of these next season. Anticipating of course that I survive this Winter, as I fear many old people will not. If not, I trust that after the Resurrection we shall be able to grow chrysanths etc in Kingdom of Heaven. I can do quite nicely without the Pearly Gates and such things.

23 December 1984

Mild and clear, 58 degrees in shop. Cloudy and mild later. Household chores. Peter, Julia and girls called with present and card. Gave them refreshment. ED called for chat and to beg thyme and sage. Mrs J called for some chrysanths. Still mild and dry so decided on cycle ride about 2.30. Saw no-one except a smiling young lady on a cycle. No doubt she thought "Whatever brings a white haired old fool out on a cycle on a day like today?". Well I suppose one day the pitcher will make its last journey to the fountain. But if, as Job stated, the limit of men's days is set by Jehovah and beyond it we cannot pass, at least he implied that we would reach that stage and not pass before. So I hope to continue cycling until I see the notice. "TERMINUS" on life's road. Reached home before darkness fell. Still mild tonight.

5 January 1985

Cold. 45 degrees in shop. Cold all day with no sign of let-up. Spent most of time indoors. Received visit from two Jehovah's Witness rep's. Gave them refreshments. Had interesting conversation. ED called for chat. Letter in post from Pauline and David, USA. They had posted me an almanac. Not yet arrived. Witty bit on radio this morn, how one of

Gracie Fields' greatest songs "It's the biggest aspidestra in the world" orginated. Really amusing. Discovered that the back seam of my work-a-day trousers was split open. Had one hell of a job threading needle by artificial light to mend it. So!

Poor old William ripped his pants and could not thread the cotton,
But he had to mend the seam tonight or get a frozen bottom.
But it's no go for the pants tonight, it's come to a sorry pass;
Unless they are patched by Monday morn I shall have a cold in my ass.

7 January 1985

The reader can relax. Old William did mend his trousers, so did not have to go down village with shirt showing. Very cold morning. 48 degrees in shop with radiator on. Light snowfall overnight. Dry all day but temperature below freezing. Weekly wash. Had mishap with machine. Waste pipe broke at junction with unit. S came up and took sheet to dry. Managed other items by hand wringing. J called for broken parts. Very cold tonight.

19 January 1985

Much warmer and better weather forecast. 48 degrees in shop with radiator on. After household chores, cleared snow from drive and pavement. Again no ''Guardian'' or racing. After lunch — rested for time, then went with J&S to visit Pat in Bromley House. Found her very cheerful. Story on radio of American firm who hope to start service of scattering one's ashes after death in outer space. Not so sure I like this. If there are any inhabitants in outer space, why should they be bothered with human filth? Better to turn our remains into fertilizer and nourish the earth which has nourished us. To plunge into the depths of fantasy, I may say that I hope to escape death and be on this earth when Shiloh comes (cf St Paul's writing). If my fate is otherwise, well so be it. I could ask Jehovah if He would let me have my old body to feed chrysanths, geraniums etc in the Kingdom of Heaven. Much as I would appreciate that, no doubt by then my executors would have disposed of my remains in a civilised manner. Always assuming of course I am accounted worthy of attaining the K of H.

20 January 1985

Milder. 48 degrees in shop. Milder all day and outlook good. Sad news this evening. Brian next door called in to tell me that his father, my good friend ED, had died at home. I was shocked and dismayed. He was with me just after noonday and we laughed and joked together about times past like a couple of schoolboys. Such is life and death. Spent afternoon clearing my bedroom ready for J to start decorating tomorrow. Too tired to take a walk afterwards. No frost tonight.

21 January 1985

Mild and wet. 50 degrees in shop. Mild all day. Snow mostly gone. Arose early. Weekly wash etc. J came to start decorating bedroom. Must sleep downstairs tonight on camp bed. Cannot grasp that ED is dead. Half expect to see him come through gates. Alas in vain:

> For no — already has his death bell rung,
> The joys of all his life are said and sung.

Thaw continues. Shall be able to cycle again soon.

26 January 1985

Milder. 50 degrees in shop without radiator on. Arose late after rather bad night. Made mistake of having chocolate milk drink for supper last night. It produced bad dreams and a head this morning like to a rotten turnip. Cleared up by midday. Afternoon went to well-attended funeral service of my good friend ED. Good address. Sang three hymns: 'Lead us, Heavenly Father, Lead us', 'The Old Rugged Cross' and 'Guide me O Thou Great Redeemer'. Now the first and third are favourite songs of mine and appropriate to the occasion, but the other always seems to me somewhat silly. It gives one the impression that when the Kingdom of Heaven does arrive on earth all who make the grade will be walking about wearing golden crowns. The height of absurdity and quite contrary to the teachings and vision of the prophets and Christ Himself. They envisaged a world of perfect peace and happiness entirely free from the three D's: Death, Disease and Deprivation. "And they that sleep in the dust of the earth shall awake and the sea give up its dead" sounds better to my rather restricted senses. Took long walk in late afternoon returning home as night was falling. A crescent moon shining in a clear cold sky — a reminder that Winter is still with us. I had by then a fine hunger, having had for lunch only a dish of soup. So enjoyed some toasted crumpets with lots of butter and cheese and a large slice of S's cake. Frost forecast again for tonight.

10 February 1985

Very cold with drifting snow. 45 degrees in shop with radiator on. Roads in bad condition especially pavements. Brought more plants down from greenhouse and did all possible to protect others. If frost continues will have to stack more in old shop. Only time out — down to J&S for dinner. Time passes tolerably well with paperbacks etc and usually good programmes on radio and TV. During very cold weather one is called upon to relieve the bladder more often and this, for men with many layers of clothes, can be a problem. Perhaps wearing a kilt would be the answer. This brings to mind a remark made to me during my young and not so innocent army days by an old Scottish sergeant. He said "Laddie, for immorality and inebriation the kilt is the finest garment in the world." Quite so. But I hardly see myself strutting down the road wearing one!

9 March 1985

Milder but rather dull. 45 degrees in shop. Milder all day. Household chores. Gave kitchen a real clean out. Gets rather dusty. Better when finished with fires perhaps. It appears to have been a long dreary Winter and time clamps down on one. In danger of becoming morbid and depressed especially since ED passed on. No daily natter and laughs. Shall have to find other interests. Peoples and races die out and are extinguished not because they are conquered and defeated but when they accept defeat, become despairing and lose excitement about the future. This is also true of individuals. A sort of hopeless attitude sets in and can become a kind of subconscious suicide or death wish. I have seen it happen. It must not happen to me. If the Eternal indeed made man in His own image (spiritually not physically), this means that man has the power within himself — given the will — to conquer defeat, taking Christ as an example. A saying I read somewhere: "It has to become dark before one can see the stars".

Started a few lettuce and marigold seeds in prop frame.

5 April 1985

Dull and cool. 51 degrees in shop. Dry during early hours, so prepared patch of garden for onion sets. Cleaned and put fertilizer around gooseberries and redcurrant. Rain came 4pm. Retired to greenhouse. Set half packet each of brussels sprouts, cabbage and cauliflower. Put out seed potatoes in boxes. Had to retire indoors shortly after 5pm. Question asked on "Any Questions" tonight: "What does Easter mean to you?" Many opinions. For myself, I think it is foolish to continue celebrating Easter as we do. Christ was murdered by His own countrymen and came forth again from death as a spiritual being able to materialise at will. Of this there is ample evidence and it was foretold by the prophets hundreds of years before. He has resided in the spiritual world with His Father now for nearly two thousand years (two days eternal time). Both Christ and the prophets foretold that in due time Christ would return to this world with power and glory to rule with justice and peace, also the signs and portents of what would happen immediately beforehand. That time is now with us for any discerning person to see. "Behold, I come as a thief. Blessed is he that watcheth and keepeth his garments lest he walk naked, and they see his shame." That is what Easter means to me.

21 April 1985

Cold bleak morning. 50 degrees in shop. Very stormy and cold NE wind. Uncanny the way this period of cold weather comes when plum and blackthorn are in bloom. Somewhere in dim recesses of my mind there is part of a poem mentioning this "blossom on the blackthorn". Now, if I shut down my conscious mind for a moment and let the subconscious take over I shall get it. Ah! here it is. In the second part of "The May Queen". Little black eyed Alice, who had been so vain the previous May when chosen as May Queen, had contracted TB. She said to her mother: "The New-year's coming up, mother, but I shall never see the blossom on the blackthorn, the leaf upon the tree." She must have survived however, for a line in the third episode runs: "To die before the snowdrop came, and now the violet's here." Nostalgia. Memories. It must be nearly eighty years since I was kept in after school hours and made to learn that poem by heart for asking cheeky questions of the teacher. No trouble. My memory was so good then I only had to read it twice and there it was. Another time it was the 91st Psalm. Same effect. They and others are still stored in my subconscious and, given the right conditions, can be called up at will. Shakespeare rightly wrote "More things in heaven and earth etc". But to return to today. Weather improved during evening. So, after watching "Highway" and "Mastermind" on TV, took sharp walk for half hour or so. Felt refreshed and enlivened by the cool air.

29 April 1985

Still cold. 48 degrees in shop. Arose early. Usual Monday morn chores. Weekly laundry. Down village to pay for last week's papers and collect pension. Three "Guardians" short last week. Mentally I calculated result in three seconds — £2.58 minus 75 = £1.83. Shopkeeper, using till, took 30 seconds and erased twice. So much for modern education. Remained cold but dry most of day.

25 May 1985

Dull and warm. Sunshine later. 60 degrees in shop. Felt rather useless. So, after seeing to housework and flowers, settled in easy chair with "Guardian". After one hour the old restlessness took over, so went outside for a spell of weeding in garden. Weeds were flourishing after recent rain. Spirits picked up, if that is the correct phrase, which goes to prove I suppose that mind controls matter. Was driven indoors again after forty minutes by heavy storm. Cleaned up and changed into lighter underclothes. Feel livelier but must admit starting to suffer the debilities of old age. Decide to ease up on some activities. Afternoon, went with J&S to visit Pat in hospital. Found her sitting in chair but not very clear in mind. It bruises my soul to see her and others all over the country who have lived a long, useful, healthy life to come to this. Waiting, waiting, waiting to be released by death. Oh God, sinful though we may be, if we are indeed made in your image, why do you treat us so? And oh Lord my God, if it is your will that I am parted from my earthly body before the return of your Son to take over the rulership of this planet, then I beseech you in your mercy let the parting be quick. The reader — if such there ever be — may think that I am a mournful sad man. Not so. I rejoice with other men, but discern life more than most. As was at one time on the cover of the periodical 'John Bull' — "Without or with offence, to friend or foe, I sketch your world exactly as it goes".

15 June 1985

Cool at first. 58 degrees in shop. Soon warmed up with sunny intervals. Was rather livelier than usual in mind and body. So, after household chores, gave workshop a tidy up — cleared all rubbish and scrap timber. Satisfied with that, made cup of mid-morning coffee and enjoyed it in my now cleaned-up back porch. I appear to have undergone a change of personality since my 89th birth date; or could be a gradual change of outlook since ED died or vacated this earthly tabernacle or to quote 'Omar' "was sold for nothing by the Broker of Hope", whichever term the reader — if such there ever be — prefers. Anyway, where once I revelled in work or any vigorous activity, I now prefer to sit in a warm place to read, write or contemplate. A passing phase? I know not. Time will tell. Planted out some more geraniums. Have been reading a book of old Shropshire houses — articles on Berwick Hall and Marrington Hall near Churchstoke, Mont., both of which I have knowledge of. Berwick Hall was taken over by Harry Hotspur as his HQ before the Battle of Shrewsbury on 21st July 1403 (in which he was slain after being deserted by his Welsh allies) and was the setting for the fulfilment of two remarkable prophecies. Marrington Hall is Elizabethan and built in 1595. A fine example. During the 1930s I dismantled a Keeper's Cottage at the brook side at the bottom of Marrington Dingle. Surrounded by woods, it must have been a weird and lonely habitation. I caught a three foot eel in the brook but, disliking them, threw it back. In the cottage were two oak windows with oak mullions and transoms. I purchased these from the builder and later fixed them in a timbered cottage I bought at Asterley. The present owner has removed them.

22 June 1985

Damp cool morning. 58 degrees in shop. Light rain and cool all day. Missing visa and passport needed for forthcoming holiday arrived by morning post. Much relieved. Over-anxiety had caused disturbed sleep and loss of appetite. No doubt one of the fruits of old age. No-one I suppose can really understand the problems of old age until one reaches that state oneself. Perhaps I myself during my long life have at times been unsympathetic to the weaknesses of the old, but I hope it has not been too obvious. Not that I have known many people to reach my age. All my contemporaries died in their sixties and seventies and some even younger and, to quote the prophet Elijah, "I even I only am left". Well, any student of the Bible will know how the Eternal smacked him down over that. To resume. After light breakfast and lunch, a bath and change and undisturbed nap by front room fire, returned to normal self. Paid outstanding account on milk and papers.

23 July 1985

Dry and sunny. Wind dropped. 60 degrees in shop. After disposing of household chores and ironing yesterday's wash, settled in back porch for rest. Girl next door bought log of timber to be shaped to make box. The things children bring to me. I must be the "Wizard of Oz". Then, as I was picking fruit, Billy (Mrs J's grandson) expressed a desire for a raspberry. After I gave him one, he put it in his mouth than spat it out and said "I don't like it very much." The honesty of children. A pity grown ups do not come as clean. Warm day forecast for tomorrow, but rain and thunder for Thursday.

25 July 1985

Very warm and humid. 69 degrees in shop and very warm all day. Health much improved and felt fairly happy, but abjured work of any kind. Sat in back porch and had conflab with self. Decided 2-0 that enough was enough; that for nearly ninety years my body had been ill-treated by myself, by world and by all my former employers; that in future I would do little but keep home and garden reasonably clean and tidy. So settled down for very easy day. Picked quantity of raspberries but have no use for them. Freezer full to door.

16 August 1985

Weather as usual. 60 degrees in shop. Heavy storms during morning. Mostly dry afternoon. Health much improved. Ripped out one row of peas and obtained few more bags for freezer. Have room now to plant out a few leeks for Spring. Letter from C&F in post. Replied immediately as this was two in row from them. Natty little tale in today's diary column of "Guardian". A man asked his friend, who was a fanatical golfer, how he managed during Winter with the frost and snow. "Oh, no problem" replied the friend "I just paint my balls orange and carry on as usual". Well, well I often wondered how I could cut down on Winter fuel bills.

23 August 1985

Dry and bright most of day. 60 degrees in shop. Neighbours next door departed on holiday to Weston-S-Mare. Left me in charge of dog, cat and fish in pond. This, with own housework, occupies more than half the day in my slowed down state. Much better today and breathing easier. Peter Julia and two girls called this morning. Gave them refreshments. Two girls found they could make merry-go-round with my pedestal easy chair. Took a mile walk without discomfort. Had a curious real life dream last night concerning life immediately after demob from First World War. Morning service and holy communion at More church. A friendship (not romantic) with a girl I have no recollection of ever meeting, but so real I would recognise her anywhere. Awoke to fact I was old man of 90 and a widower. Must relate it to Ad at the Resurrection, with other funny stories. Several starlings feeding on my bird table. Omen of early Winter? Bob phoned to say thanks for birthday card. Stephanie also had a few words.

28 August 1985

As yesterday, but more cloud and strong breeze. Usual chores for self and neighbour. Rest of morning cooking chicken to eat cold for Win's and my lunch tomorrow. Saved two legs for tea on Friday. Also cooked beef steak and fried potatoes for own lunch today. Did a little digging in garden, but tire easily now. Still, plenty of time. Amnesty Int. bi-monthly magazine in post. Tales of torture, killings and false imprisonment. Seem worse with every issue. How much longer? Picked out a box of cabbage seedlings for cutting next Spring.

30 August 1985

Fine and warm, slight breeze. 62 degrees in shop. Air close and warm. Usual chores for self and neighbour. Tomorrow last day of August. Sunday first day of September. As I sit here surrounded by semi-luxury, all and more of my needs supplied, complaining of my failing strength and contemplating the start of my 90th Winter on this earth, I ponder a while on what life would have been like in that first Winter of 1896. A husband who had to be at the pit head for 6am to descend into the bowels of the earth to earn the meagre wages paid at that time; sheep and cattle to feed, clean and milk often in driving, drifting snow; three squawking daughters aged three years, five and seven or eight, a complaining granny and lastly myself — no doubt a puny babe of six months or so whimpering to suck at breasts half the time dry through poverty. I know I was breast fed. She told me often in later life that she believed in the adage that it was preferable to feed one child over-long at the breast than carry another in the womb.

Merciful God, if God indeed is merciful (which in this present world — where the evil flourish and the poor perish — seems doubtful) if I were placed in her situation I am afraid I should contemplate mass murder and suicide. Small wonder she died worn out at sixty nine. Jim called by for tea.

1 October 1985

Arose late. 69 degrees in shop. Must have been warmest night this year and possibly the warmest October night this century. Official records will tell. It was the sort of heat which saps the energy of old men, fills them with lassitude and an overwhelming desire to rest. Nevertheless, overcame this and ironed yesterday's wash. Repaired dripping tap. Took a few cuttings of budlia and geraniums and did one or two other light jobs. This is also one of my two weekly nights to visit the "local", or one of them, to cool off. This is something I can become lyrical about and offend no-one.

The village inn, that happy place,
So pleasant free and full of grace;
The meeting place of village life
Where man can sit beside his wife,
While next to them a pair of lovers
Talk about football, sex and others.
Far more than church or village hall,
The local pub is best for all.

12 October 1985

Calm morning. Rather cold. Down to 51 degrees in shop, but compensated for by warm day later. Household chores in morning. Afternoon — two hours' tiring work in garden, including planting out wall-flowers. Was turning for bath and change and rest when C&F and David and Grace walked in. Was pleased to see them, but had very little food available, living alone. However they said "We have brought some cakes with us". So we had tea and happy two hours' natter together. They left spare cakes, a small mug from Widdicombe, a small jug for collection and box of birthday cards. A pleasant afternoon. Cyril said he was troubled with injured leg. Gave them box of raspberries and two large pots of old geranium plants still with many blossoms. Evening — 1½ hours with friends at local. Home, watched last part of musical "The King and I" on TV. A great show. For an old man, a satisfactory and interesting day. Well, as long as one discharges one's rightful duty to God and one's fellow men, all days should be good. I would that all men and women were no worse placed than myself. But remembering Amnesty International, I am afraid that many are.

13 October 1985

Cold morning. 49 degrees in shop. Warm clear day afterwards with barometer rising. Not a cloud in clear blue sky. Sends one back to childhood and innocent days when meadows, trees, hedges and the streams, the earth, the hills and everything to me did seem illumined with the light celestial. Alas, night must fall.

Usual Sunday chores, then read "Observer" until lunch J&S. Afternoon, pleasant walk up Callow Lane. Met several. Exchanged greetings or had short conversation. Back home listened to "Down Your Way" from Malvern and "Highway" with Harry Secombe from Boulogne. Last time I was in Boulogne was Summer 1918 in a casino-turned-hospital. A casualty of a bloody war. Was thereabouts for three months before returning to active service. A long time ago and little interest perhaps to anyone but self. I remember it all, even details and that the doctors were more sympathetic than the nurses, some of whom were quite vicious — and I barely 22 and come in from nearly four years of hell.

16 October 1985

Rather warm. 60 degrees in shop, but dull and cloudy day. Arose late after staying up last night reading. Miss J called for her eggs. Said she looked out on my return journey from Callow Lane to offer cup of tea. I would not be in need of the tea, but would hate to offend the old girl who is a friendly soul. Feeling rather good today. Got through several jobs. Picked and put into store one lot of apples (Lane's Prince Albert). A little more Winter digging. Washed and hung out two shirts. Was preparing bruised apples for cooking and freezing when neighbour shouted "cup of tea". Sat down with this and the addition of a little of the "elixer of life" and felt refreshed. After dinner, added one or two more verses to a poem I am writing. If these ever see the light of day the reader could get the impression that a strain of nostalgic melancholy and desire to live in the past runs through them. This is not so. While some things in the past were good, most were not — especially for the under privileged. All my hopes and desires lie in the future and the restitution of all things through Jesus Christ. Altogether a satisfying day.

Land of Lost Delight

There is a land of happy mood,
I see it ever plain;
The rugged mountains once I trod
But cannot tread again.

And from these hills of peace and joy,
Still flows a blessed air
That I remember as a boy
But now I cannot share.

This is a land of lost delight,
Of sunshine, fog and snow;
The hills and valleys once I roamed,
Where now I cannot go.

And now from memory's silent caves
I hear the curlew cry;
Could I go back but eighty years
Just once before I die

To see the blackthorn bloom again,
The pink buds on the larch,
The forest trees renew their leaves,
The sex mad hares in March.

WF

17 October 1985

Cloudy, dull morning and day. 58 degrees in shop. The kind of weather that sends old men to sleep with a wish to hibernate for the Winter. Household chores. Little of interest happened. Two letters in post. One from Amnesty International, other from Water Board — reminder of water rate. Already paid. FW called with Jehovah's Witness mag. Jim phoned. Has bad cold. Not coming out tomorrow. MEB called to read meter. Took mile or so walk before dusk. Small item in Shropshire Star about EEC giving grant toward sex education for the over sixties. This seemed to me to be extremely funny. If one has not learned to do it in a happy and relaxed manner by that age, I would submit it were better to give it up altogether and take to drink, which would be cheaper and less harmful. Had the idea of sending jokey letter to local press. Desisted in case neighbours took offence. Anyway EEC turned idea down.

9 November 1985

Clear cold morning after stormy wet night. 52 degrees in shop though cold outdoors. Usual household chores but body rebelled against anything further. Autumn is now well and truly with us. As I look from my bedroom window on a clear sunny morning, I see the tree-clad Stiperstones hills with their varied Autumn colours. The pale gold of the larch, the dark green of other conifers and the varied browns of other forest trees. The tops of the mountains silhouetted against a bank of fleecy cloud like a dark jewel resting on a pile of cotton wool. When I see these things, my heart and mind are uplifted and I render grateful thanks to the powers that control my destiny that I live and have my being in such surroundings instead of some inner city, boxed in by lifeless buildings. I know that many would not agree with me on this, preferring the hustle and bustle of city life. But I am what I am. Very quiet day with few distractions. Watched on TV — Bold Rix, with Joe Mercer up, win November Handicap (the last great flat race of the season). A fine win. Had pancake for tea. Made too much batter and could not eat it all.

10 November 1985

Cold. 45 degrees in shop. A much different scene from bedroom window. Colours on hillside still there but hilltops white with snow under leaden sky. A piercing NW wind, which chills one, especially old men. Lunch J&S. Intended a walk, but storms came so stayed indoors. Win and Judy called about 7pm. Brought me some carrots. Gave them a box of apples (Blenheims).

17 November 1985

Cold morning but the sun shines. 41 degrees in shop. Cold clear sunshine most of day. Usual Sunday morning chores, then settled with "Observer" until lunchtime with J&S. Afterwards listened to "Gardener's Question Time". Learned little except that root ginger can grow into house plant. Note. Try it sometime.

Started out for a walk about 3.15 in the bright Autumn sunshine. The Dorricotts were at Miss D's cottage. Had a few words with them. Carried on up Callow Hill road. Exchanged greetings with one or two others. Reached Bank Farm and beyond. The sun was now setting behind a bank of clouds which, to an imaginative observer, would seem to be a range of silver-topped mountains interspersed with flame-coloured lakes in the far distance. One could almost wish that one could wear the magic winged sandals of Jason of Greek mythology as he travelled to the abode of the gods to retrieve the Golden Fleece. Were I so equipped however I would let the Golden Fleece lie and fly on into infinity never to return. Taking a saner view though, this would place an intolerable burden on my executors who would have to presume my death. Better to leave things as they are. On return home, darkness was falling, also a cold damp mist — but a crescent moon shone in a clear sky above. Was glad of a glass of sherry and the fireside. Listened with a joyous heart to "Down Your Way" and "Highway" with Harry Secombe. A thick mist now covers everything.

26 November 1985

Cold but clear sunshine for a couple of hours. 42 degrees in shop. Had slight return of lung congestion I suffered last Summer. No doubt through too much time indoors. Cleared up shortly after midday. Miss J called for her eggs and left me a few mince pies. A treat. Story on radio, before midday News, of lady who had a nightingale at bottom of her garden and wished to make a record of its notes accompanied by herself on violin. Did so with good results, but somewhere along the line a young donkey and a motor ambulance on a nearby road also joined in. The best experience I ever had with nightingales was early Summer 1917 near Kemmel on the Western Front. I was in charge of a signal station in a redoubt in a wood about half a kilometer behind the front line (called Bois Redoubt) and occupied by a company of infantry. There must have been several pairs of nightingales there. My turn of duty was usually 8pm till 4am and from the edge of darkness onwards the air would be full of their music. It filled me with wonder and ecstasy to think that this could happen just a few hundred yards from where death and destruction were regular occurrences. Sad to relate, the day after we were relieved the whole place was destroyed by enemy artillery. Poor nightingales. Poor me, had I still been there. A case of "The earth returned to earth as it was" — and the spirit? But here am I, by the grace of the Eternal, nearly seventy years after living it all over again. Weather continues cold. Snow forecast for most districts tonight. A long way from my nightingales and Bois Redoubt.

28 December 1985

Very cold and dry after severe night frost. 40 degrees in shop with radiator on. Everyone apparently staying indoors. Only saw and exchanged greetings with two or three people. Interesting programme on BBC2 about Great Western Railway and Brunel and his life and times. When this one-time great country of ours led the world in engineering, we built railways the world over and supplied the rolling stock and power units for them. We made the first camera, the first steam ship and the first screw-driven one. Admittedly its workforce were poorly rewarded for their labours, but the brain and brawn and courage were British and the name was enough. Pathetic though it may be, we now have to depend for a large part of our foreign exchange on visitors from more prosperous countries who come to stare at our decaying mansions and castles and gawp at that dolled up and decorated goon show called the Royal Family. But somewhere within our nation there is, I am sure, a vast reservoir of courage and resource waiting to be tapped by the right leader. No mail today and very cold tonight. Finished evening at local. Home 11.30. Bright and cold night.

2 January 1986

A damp dull day from the start. 40 degrees in shop. Rain fell most of time until well after nightfall. Win came out. Cooked good lunch. Changed library books. One entitled "Along the Green Roads of Britain". Story of byways from centuries ago until present. I would say that walking the byways resembles the journey through life. There is much more of interest to be found along the way than at the end, however pleasant that end may be. It is better to dawdle and taste the joys or pain of each passing moment than hurry recklessly to one's destruction. Most of us discover this truth too late, for time erases all. So let me live my life. That delightful programme "Treasure Hunt" returned to Channel 4 tonight. Set in North Wales.

25 January 1986

Cold and clear. Sun shining. Frost last night. 42 degrees in shop with radiator on. Usual household chores. Because of cold wind was disinclined to move far from home. Idleness seems to be becoming a way of life, no doubt as for many more old people. Well, we wait for better times. Some poet once wrote (sounds like Browning or Shelley) "They also serve who only stand and wait". I would remark here that a wise person would not stand and wait but take the weight off the feet and sit. This I did, having several vacant easy chairs. All that is lacking is a friendly person to converse with while waiting. One thing I enjoy very much of a Saturday evening is sitting back in an easy chair in front of a good fire with closed eyes and listening to "Baker's Dozen". A pleasure indeed and relaxing. How many homeless people sleeping rough would like to change places? Had simple meals today. Only cooking — made custard to go with fruit for tea.

31 January 1986

Glad to see January out. A rather miserable wet month, but not too cold. Wet morning and indeed light rain continued all day. 42 degrees in shop. Awoke well before 8am. Crept downstairs in dressing gown and slippers. Drew curtains back in old shop. Fetched in week's supply of milk, then crept back to still warm bed and let the rain carry on. From an article in today's "Guardian" about food, I learn that the plant we call sow thistle and look upon as an obnoxious weed is indeed good for one as an additive to soups or a mixed salad, also a medicine. It is rich both in minerals and vitamin C. In Greek mythology the hero Theseus slew the minotaur after consuming a dish of them and afterwards wed the Queen of the Amazons. Must have been a bit of a lad. For, if Greek history is true, he would not be up to slaying anything and would need a stronger diet than sow thistles after a few nights in bed with her. Well I have no wish to marry a Queen, but I will give the plant a small trial come Summer.

2 April 1986

Cold dry morning after cold night. 50 degrees in shop with radiator on. After morning tea, got off to a bad start. First mislaid keys of workshop and building. Was somewhat upset, perhaps unnecessarily so. Found them on floor of old shop. Must have dropped them when setting up radiator last night. Later, when chopping morning sticks, axe slipped. Had it been sharp, I would have been minus one inch of left thumb. Being blunt, got a bad bruise. The end result however was beneficient. I lost my calm, the adrenalin started flowing. Told myself I was a nit-witted, stupid, awkward fool not fit to be let out alone. Bound thumb with Elastoplast and, when pain subsided, felt much better. I wonder whether the Prince of Wales reacted in the same way when he injured his finger last week. I doubt it. He would surely have had six first-aid people, a doctor and a nurse falling over each other to assist. Three letters in the post. One from Bank stating that in future they would open for business on Saturday mornings. One from nephew Doug in Cheddar saying a whole new series of caves had been discovered beneath the Mendips and one from nephew and niece, David and Pauline, giving their new address. Still in Arizona. Temp there 83 degrees in shade — and poor us shivering around freezing point. Weather improved after lunch, so had two hours outside in garden. Cleaned and loosened soil in flower bed and prepared site for onion sets.

16 April 1986

Arose early, feeling quite lively and alert. No doubt on account of beer I consumed last night. 49 degrees in shop. Regular rain which continued until late afternoon. Rather than sit in house moping, decided to visit Shrewsbury. Did so. Paid local rates. Had haircut. Made several purchases. Price of haircut risen by 15p since last time. Felt in need of some sustenance so bought cup of tea at riverside cafe. 39p. Oh dear. Took regular cheque to Oxfam. Purchased two smashing ties (as new) there. 25p each. Delighted. Returned home midday bus. A man came and sat by me with a walking stick. Said he was 82 and still going strong. Congratulated him on his vigour and young looks. Asked him how he did it, but did not tell him I was eight years older than that. Well, we all have our moments. House cold on return home, so made fire in front room. Enjoyed cold lunch. FW called with Jehovah's Witness mag. Gave him refreshments. Later, Julia and Heather called. Made tea and biscuits for self and them. Bank statement in post. Healthy.

30 May 1986

Fine and warm. 59 degrees in shop, 72 degrees later. Wind much calmer, which gave a pleasant day. Got out quite a few bedding plants in tubs and borders. Phone call from lady. Would like to see over Miss D's house about 3.30. Told her OK. Duly arrived. An up and coming divorcee with no inhibitions. Said she would like the house. In answer to query, said her name was Jenny B---- and she now lived at Pennerley. Told her I knew the district and that if she came to Minsterley I would soon find her a fresh hubby. Laughed and said she was alright and had two dogs for company. Small respect for men. Well, too old myself at 90 anyway.

13 June 1986

And it is Friday 13th. Warm and humid. 62 degrees in shop. Restless night caused by severe head and chest cold. In morning was undecided whether to stay in bed and pray for death or arise and fight. However, remembered that the week's milk supply would be on the doorstep; also that I had to take a suit to the agency for the cleaners; also must take frozen chicken out of freezer for tea this evening. So, struggled and arose.

So it's no go for death today,
It's no go for glory;
All I need is a bottle of Scotch
And a woman to tell me a story.

Made the village after a pot of tea. Purchased two large lemons and made strong lemon drink. Am now awaiting the results. Will the Diary end here or not? Just received and somewhat enjoyed "meals on wheels". Boiled ham and three veg and apple crumble. Chances of survival now 50/50. Jim called by for tea. Temp in shop reached 82. Wall flower seed germinated in greenhouse.

26 June 1986

Warmest yet. 70 degrees in shop. A morning at least to enjoy perfect idleness. This I am doing. Forecast says fine weather will only last two days. So, let the very old (meaning self) revel in that carefree idleness which was denied them in their youth and to hell with tomorrow. Temperature reached 82 degrees later. Picture late on BBC1 of Battle of Somme 1916. The greatest disaster and horror that ever overtook any British army at any time. All owing entirely to the incompetence, stupidity and dull wittedness of the British High Command — all at that time drawn from public school class. Watched for a time but soon had a bellyfull of the evils of a past age. Returned to bed only to be tormented by souls of dead comrades and pictures of the stinking, blackened, maggot-infested, rat-eaten bodies of men of all nations, passing before me like pictures on a screen. They were forever rising up and pointing, pointing, pointing with skeleton fingers at a great black cloud rushing towards us from the horizon. Slept at last and soundly. Why my life was spared I know not. Suffice it to say it was.

30 June 1986

Warm, humid and dull. 70 degrees in shop. Cool wind outside. Usual Monday morning jobs then easy going until afternoon. Made Shrewsbury on 1.25 bus. Few travellers. Streets quiet and cool. Was quite comfortable but did not stay long. Caught 3pm bus back home. Humidity and temperature high this evening. Had a quantity of old potatoes and patch of spare ground in garden, so made use of them both, for my future benefit (I hope). Much ado in religious circles lately about the ordination of women. For myself I cannot see why women (who on average have more intelligence, intuition and forward-looking ideas) should wish to join a class of men, 75% of whom hold the job not for any religious conviction but for lack of ability to hold down any other. Jesus was not ordained by some ridiculous big-wig. Indeed He poured scorn and ridicule with good effect on the priesthood of His day who, like those of the present, were steeped in ritual and dogma and the desire to parade in funny clothes. Because of this, they failed to see in Christ the embodiment and manifestation of the love of God for man and the ultimate salvation of any who cared to hear and believe. The Roman church, more than any, is tied to politics and power. If women want real power, they should cry out loud to men to come into the light (instead of craving to enter the aisles of darkness themselves). Wrote and posted letter to "Poetry Please", BBC with a request. Bought a packet of early peas for late sowing.

7 July 1986

62 degrees in shop, with slight breeze outside, Max 75 later. Usual Monday duties. Had idea to visit Shrewsbury during afternoon but, owing to tiredness and failing eyesight, postponed it until tomorrow. On second visit down village for supplies, met lady in shop who also spent her childhood among the Stiperstones. During conversation I said I would like to be up there again during this hot weather with a tent and ample supplies — to set up camp by one of the pure springs that I know and live in solitude and peace for a few days. No doubt I would soon tire of it, but a nice thought. Had one or two hours redecorating Summer House. Have too much junk and furniture in it. Must be rid of some, even if it means a fire when garden is cleared. Have eaten little today so will prepare a good evening meal.

Shropshire

Delightful shire where beauty reigns
With flowers choicest sweet
And fair does shine your northern plain
Where wealth and beauty meet.

Filled am I with poetic fire
When Shropshire is my theme
And strike sweet music from the lyre
With notes of ardent beam.

Sweet nature cleans your fragrant air
And every breath is health.
Your hills and valleys, oh how fair,
Their beauty is your wealth.

Oh let me here with beauty stray
And climb yon lovely hill;
Let nature all her charms display,
My soul with music fill.

Oh let me see with shining eyes
Some lovely Summer even,
Your hills that meet the bluest skies
And lose their tops in heaven.

Your fields, by nature's bounty bound,
Are dressed in vivid green
And hamlets that the fields surround
Complete the varied scene.

A walk beneath your shady trees
Shuts out all earthly strife
And Summer's enervating breeze
Restores all things to life.

The buildings of your county town
Delight my roving eye;
How calm the waters flowing down,
The Severn passing by.

What happiness is brings to roam
The Clee and Stretton hills,
While Wenlock Edge and Wenlock town
The soul with rapture fills.

To stand alone on Long Mynd's height
Upon a Summer morn
When, with the passing of the night,
Another day is born.

Or climb once more to Rhadley's rock
And get a gracious sight
Of mists that rise from Onny Brook
As dawn defeats the night.

Were I with Moses when he sat
The Promised Land to view
And had the choice of this or that,
I would have chosen you.

The perfume of your scented woods
And of your verdant dales,
They match the ever-changing moods
That nature's law entails.

From Cambria's hills to Wrekin mound,
From Ludlow to the Dee,
No fairer land was ever found
Nor will there ever be.

And if the times be good or bad
Or pain or pleasure bring,
I'd rather be a Shropshire lad
Than reign an Arab king.

WF

Footnote: The foregoing is really drivel. I do love Shropshire, especially its hills. The trouble is — most of its dwellers are conservative, wishing to stay in the present or live again in the past.

Stiperstones — The Devil's Chair

9 July 1986

Still dry. Slightly cooler and cloudy. Reached only 70 degrees later. Stayed around home and garden all day. In spite of drought, weeds persist. Cleared two portions today. Will make bonfire in day or two if drought continues. Redcurrants and some peas ready for picking. A job for tomorrow. Dug a root of own potatoes for my evening meal. Very good. During this Summer weather and the loneliness of old age, one's thoughts revert to the days of one's childhood, remembering the good things and forgetting the bad. I see a long cool dairy with one or two barrels of home-brewed beer on stands and a horn drinking cup upside down on one. A long shelf with shallow pans of milk, skimmed or waiting to be skimmed (this was before separators were in general use), a large dish of cold boiled potatoes to be taken at will when hungry, another of cold rice or bread pudding with stacks of raisins in it — also a hunger satisfier for young bellies. I had a thousand acres of mountain and moorland and field to wander in, with one rule only to be strictly observed (shut all gates after passing through), one hundred springs of pure water to satisfy a thirst and above all the pure air of heaven. One forgets the bad, or tries to. The lack of money — a penny was a fortune — the patched clothes, the darned socks and shoes with worn out soles. After all, one's neighbours were perhaps worse off. One forgets the midden in the yard and the smelly earth closet. A boy did not need the latter during six months of the year anyway. He could drop his short trousers, without being observed, under a hedge in the bracken or heather and a large leaf or bracken frond or grass served as toilet paper and nature saw to it afterwards. I can here see my grandchildren and great grandchildren looking horrified. But poof, I was free. Whilst they are, and now I also am, tied to the wheels of convention. Ah well, who is the winner or the loser? Better a dinner of herbs etc.

29 July 1986

Temperature as yesterday, 65 degrees in shop. Heavy rain during night, but more needed. Some sunshine later in day. Made journey to Shrewsbury on 12.30 bus to settle MEB account and several other bits and pieces. Only one other person on bus when I boarded it and less than half full when reached destination. No person or event of interest on journey. Spent most of time thinking up imaginary exploits for my mythical Irish ancester, supposedly killed at Battle of Waterloo. Was so engrossed in the humorous yarns that I was on point of bursting into laughter when I realised where I was and camouflaged it with a fit of coughing. Lady behind was concerned and asked was I alright. Explained I must have swallowed a fly. Poor old ancestor. Well, he was Irish. Kept busy with this and that. Returned 3pm bus. After cup of tea, laid new carpet in Summer House and put back furniture. Rearrange tomorrow. By now extremely tired, so prepared evening meal and settled in chair. Article on radio at 7.20 about life and works of Shropshire writer Mary Webb, who one time lived in this locality. To me, Mary Webb was a tragic figure. No joy whatever in her books. She could have been mirror ing her own life in her writings — an over-bearing mother, her own suffering from Grave's disease and never knowing the joys of motherhood.

19 August 1986

Cool and dry. 58 degrees in shop. Reached 68 later. Dry all day with much sunshine. Put more runner beans in freezer. Sorted out some plants and bulbs in top greenhouse. Pleased with condition of maidenhair ferns. M next door brought me back a plant from holiday — a 'Cordyline' or Dragon Tree. Much appreciated. Evenings now have the feel of Autumn. Improved later. Returned home from pub (drink and dominoes) 11pm. A calm, cloudless, windless night. Full moon shining low in the southern sky. Was reminded of times of peace and tranquility of 80 90 years ago, before the days of combine harvesters. Farm folk in those days carried home the sheaves by light of harvest moon up until midnight or after and then gorged themselves with pure home-produced food and drink. Then the scene changed, I saw the abject poverty of the workers and the pitiless ending of a noble life in a comfortless workhouse and thought "No, a thousand times no. Better today with all its evils than a return to that." We need no Grey writing an 'Elegy of a Country Churchyard' of our times or a Robert Bloomfield's 'Farmer's Boy', however possible it may be that a worse fate could overtake us.

30 September 1986

Continuing the warmth and idleness of yesterday. 58 degrees in shop. After a night of thick warm fog — ideal for September — the sun eventually broke through about 10am. I now sit in the warmth and comfort of my glass porch, resting as I pursue my leisurely and lonely way to the Jordan. Hoping — no doubt with many others — that the crossing will not be too deep or too cold. I seldom have cold feet anyway. Interlude here as I answer phone. Someone to view Miss D's cottage. 12.30 OK? To resume. As a small boy we had a Family Bible with a bright picture in it of an old man with beard and long hair standing on high ground with his hand shading his eyes. Title 'Moses viewing the Promised Land'. Must have looked good to him. But what I remember most of all was the brightness of his robes. Pure white and brilliant red. Must have had a good laundry maid to come up like that without the aid of Persil or Ariel etc. Procter and Gamble had not then started business, but I believe what we know as Common Soda was plentiful.

So, there we are. If Moses was not allowed to cross the Jordan, at least he died in a clean shirt. May I be allowed the same blessing. Well, blessings are comparative. Following short poem read in today's "Guardian", copied from London Tube:

Western wind when wilt thou blow,
The small rain down can rain;
Christ, if my love were in my arms
And I in bed again.

A heartcry no doubt from someone who had to rise early after a night out. Moral for the young — if warm September nights, a full moon and romance are good companions; late nights, early rising and romance are not.

Another interlude. Young couple to have further look at cottage. Bright picture in my one flower bed. Michaelmas Daisies (dwarf) and red geraniums in a perfect mixture. One of the joys of life for rich and poor alike, with an added pleasure for the one who tends them.

5 October 1986

Warm and dull. 60 degrees in shop. Feeling rather worn out and tired. Usual Sunday chores. Stayed around home most of day except dinner J&S. Afternoon watched racing from Longchamp on TV. Saw Pat Eddery on Dancing Brave score a fine victory. Article in today's "Observer" — crematorium plans to use warmth from burning bodies to help heat building. A commendable idea. But, without appearing to joke on the subject, I would submit that if this is done the deceased's executors should have a discount on the fee. The fatter the corpse, the greater the discount. I am thin, so forget it.

5 November 1986

Cold and cloudy. 50 degrees in shop, but cold, uncomfortable day outdoors. Did little but household chores. Called coal merchant and ordered 5 cwt Coalite — or rather equivalent in kilos — for next Monday. One journey down village. Purchased bottle Advocaat £5.20. Do for special visitors, too costly to drink myself. Made excellent stew for midday. Mince with several veg etc. from freezer and garden. Estimated it would make two meals but it was so good scoffed the lot and suffered all afternoon. Pughs of Asterley have just phoned. They would fetch me tomorrow afternoon to see the village once more. Good old Asterley. Spent thirty one years there (including War years). Most of them very happy. Well, the philosopher said, I forget which one, quote "Life is a bridge, pass over it but do not build a house upon it'' unquote. Sound advice. In today's ''Guardian'', advert for life assurance reads ''If you die you get instant cash''. Oh! I always had the impression that you could not take it with you. Perhaps the rules have been altered. As I see it, the only thing one could be sure of taking with one would be a full stomach (even that would be in danger of a Post Mortem).

So, let us pray for a good appetite on the morning of the Great Day.

So, we will drink a toast to life today
And the Devil take tomorrow;
All a man needs is jolly good food
And a drink to drown his sorrows.

Cheers!

6 November 1986

Cold and clear. 42 degrees in shop. Near frost outdoors. Bracing air and clear skies. Usual chores then idle morning. MP called for visit to Asterley 2pm. Lasted two hours or so. Met and talked to old friends. Very enjoyable afternoon. Good will everywhere. Village much improved with new bungalows and better housing.

13 November 1986

Mild and wet. 52 degrees in shop. Became colder later. Rain continued until after 3pm. Had symptoms of developing cold, so stayed indoors most of day. Passed word of greeting with one neighbour and the coupon collector. Time passed pleasantly enough with several activities, but if many days the same will soon be dropping into obscurity against my will. I suppose many people live in obscurity most of their lives. Take Civil Servants for example ''They spend their lives in stuffy rooms without much hope or mention. Sit on their arse for fifty years and then they live on a pension.''

But it's no go for the meek today,
It's no go for the tame ones —
A man must fight so long as he lives
For the Devil catches the lame ones.

6 December 1986

Cold night. Fine and bright and cold this morning. 40 degrees in shop. No more than 46 all day. As usual, not very lively early part of day but managed household chores and weekly laundry before luncheon. Weather bright and clear for drying purposes. Made scratch lunch of beacon and eggs and left-over fruit and rice pudding. By this time very tired, so settled in front room and watched racing from Cheltenham. A fine course and bright sunshine. In 1.40 race   Floyd, with C Brown up, led 8-10 lengths whole of course and won by clear margin. I have been contemplating planting another row of raspberry canes in garden ('Malling Jewel'). I have to consider that the canes would not come to fruition or bear fruit until June 1988. By that time I shall in all probability be ''gathered to my fathers'' as the Scriptures so often state (I wonder at this. No mention is ever made of the mothers who expend nine tenths of the necessary effort to rear any child. Male chauvinism — then as now, only more so). Also, re the raspberries, the next person here may let the garden go back to jungle or grass it down. I well remember when I sold the Asterley property. After I had spent years of hard labour transforming half an acre of nettles and jungle into a landscape of flowers, fruit and vegetables, one prospective buyer said he was estimating how many pigs he would be able to keep on it. "Then I looked on all the works that my hands had wrought, and on the labour that I had laboured to do: and behold, all was vanity and vexation of spirit, and there was no profit under the sun." Therefore there is nothing better than that a man should rejoice in his own works. For who shall know what comes after? Perhaps the silence of a wise man is better than the vapourings of a fool. While I have been writing this, my fire has burned low. Which class am I?

10 December 1986

Cold morning after cold night. 45 degrees in shop with radiator on. Hoar frost on everything. Ice on pavement and watertub. Arose rather late. Immediately, man called to view Miss D's cottage. Said former buyer had to withdraw — happened twice now. Another man called. Said he had load of fire logs for next door. Were they in? Sorted them both out and returned home. Had light breakfast. Did household chores, which included front room hearth and laying fire ready for evening. So! Entered room some time later and found, to my surprise, that fire had in some mysterious way ignited itself. Did not suppose for a moment that the prophet Elijah had visited my humble dwelling, but was not altogether displeased, outdoors being cold and uninviting. Made fire up and shut down draught. House soon became warm and cosy. Man from British Legion called later with Christmas cheque. So was able to receive him in warm room.

Turning over some of Ad's papers, found a recipe for potato fritters. Sounded simple enough, even for my small and immature mind. Will try it at tea time. Did so. Medium to good result. Would perhaps have been better using boiled mashed potatoes instead of grated ones. In trouble once more. Have worn a hole in knee of trousers and not — repeat not — through kneeling in church. A warm pair. Do not like parting company before end of Winter. Must bodge them up somehow. So, knees up Mother Brown, or rather Uncle Bill.

4 January 1987

Complete change in weather. Wet and mild. 46 degrees in shop. Rained all day until dusk. Could not even contemplate a walk. Made do with household chores, newspaper and books. Good radio and TV programmes after dark. Interesting "Down Your Way" from Cardiff. One item — a small farm in midst of a city. More interesting still, a dinosaur museum. Skeletons of course. One said to be 42 metres long. Largest known. I christened him Charlie. That would be more than half the distance from my house to the Bath Arms. Blimey! Fancy meeting Charlie at 11.30pm coming home. However, they were said to be harmless creatures so no doubt, after a few pints of good ale, I would have courage to blow down his nose (if it was a he) and make friends and not have a nightmare afterwards.

Mastermind also returns tonight.

13 January 1987

Still very cold night and day. Forecast similar. Very important to keep warm and comfortable. Stayed indoors most of time. One journey down village. Rather good lunch from "meals on wheels". Perhaps enjoyed more because cold sharpened appetite. Made some potato cakes for evening meal. Profiting from last time's mistakes, did a really good job and enjoyed excellent meal. Listening to radio today before midday News, I heard a group of people discussing old fashioned songs. One brought up the song "That Old Fashioned Mother of Mine". Said it was worn out and played out and that something should be done about the Old Fashioned Father, as it was self-evident that without the Old Fashioned Father the Old Fashioned Mother would never have become an Old Fashioned Mother. Quite so. But this cuts both ways. Without the assistance of the Old Fashioned Mother, the Old Fashioned Father would never have become an Old Fashioned Father (I hope all this is clear to the would-be reader). Therefore, as I see it, the honours are equal and the Old Fashioned Mother and the Old Fashioned Father must share the praise or the blame, whichever way you see it. Catalogue from Woolmans the chrysanth people in post. Very cold tonight.

4 April 1987

Awoke late to a dull dark morning with continual rain which persisted all day up until darkness fell. Apart from the necessity of getting food and tidying house, may just as well have spent the whole day in bed. However, did arise. Sorted things out. Had light breakfast of mixed cereal, tea and a biscuit. Main job — sorting and ironing yesterday's big wash. Came lunchtime. Tin of soup, cheese sandwich and fresh fruit. Fruit is said to be good for one. In my young days (oh so long ago) there was a Music Hall song in which "Eve said to Adam, the saucy little madam, oh Adam you must eat more fruit". He would then live to be ninety nine. He must have followed her advice, with excellent results, for according to records he lived to be nine hundred and thirty. Which goes to prove what I am always telling other men. If you wish to live a long and happy life, follow your wife's counsel. After lunch, settled down to watch racing from Aintree including Grand National. Did not appear to be raining there. 11.15pm home from enjoyable evening at Bath Arms. Still steady rain falling. Must be 24 hours now. No doubt many houses bailing out. May sit up reading and sleep late tomorrow.

6 April 1987

Awoke to a cold, wet, foggy morning and cool wind. Lost the sunshine of yester afternoon. Perhaps sun will shine through later. Meanwhile, my greatest problem is to keep my declining bodily structure 'warmed and

Bath Arms, Minsterley

fed, without the aid of joy.' It is written "Where there is no joy the people perish". I would add — where there is no joy the individual must also perish. Its ego withers and dries like an over-ripe apple in the sun, until all that remain are its seeds to perpetuate or not, according to the dictates of nature, at the place where they fall. The great Winston Churchill once said in a Christmas speech during the Second World War "It is a poor heart that never rejoices". Well, Churchill (behind his belligerent exterior) was a visionary. No doubt, however mistaken we may be, he — like myself — looked for a time when the carpet of joy and sunshine of eternal happiness would fall upon the human race. Meanwhile, such as it is, we have to abide in this world. Today, when collecting pension, purchased six Easter cards for nephews and nieces in USA. Get them off tomorrow — or so I hope. Afternoon mostly dry so managed to plant onion sets. Four rows. Thought I was late this season, but looking back in diary found I planted sets last year on April 14 and April weather was rather worse than today.

10 April 1987

Awoke normal time to a bright cold morning. Temp down to 43 degrees in shop, but no rain. Just before waking had a remarkable dream which would make the basis of a short story any magazine would be glad to accept. It was about two people I knew years ago at different stages of my life, years apart. A man in his mid forties and a girl in her early twenties. Both terminally ill and without hope. In the dream they stood together in a street holding hands and singing. What music! On awakening, my first thought was to write a short story about it and send it to a publisher. But of course I shall not. However, it could be a subject for some writer in a future age — not the Jeffrey Archer type though. Nevertheless, I must admit here I admired his story 'The First Miracle' about the Roman boy who gave his food and fruit to the mother of Christ. It proved to me that there could still be some humanity, even in the unlikely place of the mind of a Tory. More likely my dream was intended for me — to condemn my disgruntled and discontented attitude to old age. So be it. Lunch time now and sun still shines. Good lunch today from "meals on wheels". Last for two weeks because of Easter break. Afterwards turned to more practical matters. Removed several crowns from overcrowded rhubarb bed and started fresh clump ready for next year's harvest. Also started to move old compost on to garden. Two year's collection. Owing to bodily weakness, failed to move it last year. Looks very good. By 4pm had become very tired. Moved indoors for rest and refreshment. Evening became dull with some rain. Slightly warmer.

27 April 1987

Warm day materialised. 58 degrees in shop, reached 78 later. Rather tiring. Cleared up several duties. Gave kitchen good clean. No fires now and take most meals in back porch. Also cleaned porch. Journey down village. Paid for papers and collected pension. Met old lady acquaintance. Asked after her health. She said she suffered from Rheumatoid Arthritis and that she was becoming a burden. I replied that old age was a burden anytime. A thought crossed my mind later. How nice it would be if we could live for ever, or at any rate for a much longer period, in what has been the best time of our life. I would say that mine was between my sixtieth and eightieth birthday. In that period we had ample money and an abundance of good health and contentment. But for many of course this was not the case. In the Far East there was the Vietnam War and the 'killing fields'. But life goes on and departs like a story that is told and forgotten or a ship that passes in the night. Now at 92, or near so, I am like a passenger in the departure lounge of an air terminal, waiting for his flight to be called for a journey from which there is no return. But, why be cast down? Many aspects of life are still good. Planted last row of peas today, also one row of potatoes. Another fine sunset.

4 May 1987

A clear and rather cold morning. Wind not quite so bad. 50 degrees in shop, reached 65 later. Road very quiet. No sign of activity by neighbours on either side. Could be away or staying indoors for warmth. Remained in bed as long as possible. Was idle afterwards except keeping house tidy and getting simple meals. Afternoon watched spectacular film "Waterloo". Spectacular no doubt, but hardly convincing. Now, scarcely anyone will believe this — they will put it down to senility — but I must have been there in a former existence. Probably killed there. The picture firmly etched on my mind is as follows. Wellington (with HQ in Brussels) hearing the French army were on their way to attack his forces, sent out a light force under a Brig. Gen. They had orders to delay the French advance by any means other than to stand and fight and then to fall back on main position prepared meanwhile. This they did for two days. During those two days there was almost continual heavy rain (an act of God, many said). This prevented the French getting their overwhelming superiority of heavy artillery, which they used to demoralise their enemies, into position. So the Battle of Waterloo raged with all its bloodiness and horror until early evening and could be called a draw, but for a German army under Blucker which threatened the French right flank and so changed the whole scene. A bad day indeed for the French nation — a much more cultured people than us or the Germans. Still, as the tragic Madam Bovary remarked, "What will come, will come". The future of all lies in the hand of the Eternal. Who am I to scan or question it? Many no doubt will laugh at or doubt the foregoing. By then I shall be a handful of ashes.

Later now and am sitting in comfort by a cosy fire. Had a kipper for tea. A fair meal for a poor man. Well, no shame to being poor. But my drawback in life is that it was instilled into me as a child that I had to be honest (whatever that really means). As Pontius Pilate said to Christ "What is truth?" I may also ask — how do you define honesty? Looking through my 'library' for reading matter, selected a copy of "The Last Days of Pompeii". Picked up somewhere years ago for the magnificent price of 9 pence (old coinage). It appears to be an 1834 edition. Contains much Greek and Roman poetry and song. I have many such books, half read or scarcely touched. Shall I live to read them or will they be discarded by future generations as trash? God forbid. But fear not. Come fearful man, fill up the cup that clears today of past regrets and future fears. Tomorrow? Why, tomorrow I may be myself with yesterday's ten thousand years.

6 May 1987

Fine morning followed by warm day. 52 degrees in shop. Reached 74 later. Needed to attend clinic to have ears cleared of wax. So, reluctantly, rose early to catch 9.25 bus. Clinic very busy and was obliged to wait some considerable time for attention. Lady helper or nurse or whatever (a pleasant greying person) failed to remove wax at first attempt. When she returned, I quoted Shakespeare to her. "Once more unto the breach, dear friends, once more; or close the wall up with our English dead". To my surprise and delight she came back with a quotation of her own. From then on we were friends and discussed 'Macbeth', 'Henry V' etc etc. Culture or egotism on my part? 50/50 perhaps. Leaving clinic, visited Hignett's for something for dinner. Also Bank to enhance credit. Found last bus for considerable time had left, so walked home. Slight effort climbing Malehurst Bank, otherwise no trouble. Had excellent lunch of orange juice, smoked cheese, wholemeal rolls, green salad of sorts and a can of beer. Finished with tinned peaches. A cheap and satisfying meal for a hungry and poverty stricken old man. Sad to state, I did not at the time give thanks to the Eternal for healthy appetite and the means to satisfy it. I do so now and may I be forgiven. After all that, except for watering young plants, enjoyed an idle afternoon.

Sun now disappearing behind factory. Soon cool down. Best to retire indoors.

19 May 1987

Slightly warmer and calm. 52 degrees in shop. Rather more sun today, so spent some time in garden. Letter and card from David and Pauline USA in post. Small item in today's paper about widow ninety three years of age about to be married to her fifth husband. Well well, I ask you. Some talk of Alexander and some of Hercules; some of hope springing eternal in the human breast and some of the triumph of hope over experience. The lady must have all these things in mind. I congratulate her for her staying power, but reserve sympathy for the husband.

4 June 1987

A fine dry start to the day. 60 degrees in shop. However, rain fell before midday. Little to do except small items of home work. Attended to next door's cat, dog and fish. Content now to sit in warmth of back porch or old shop and dream of past and present. Future not worth bothering about. "Que Sera, Sera". Garden and all plants enjoy the rain. Freezer getting somewhat empty so gathered what herbs and veg I have from garden and made good veg stew for lunch. What wrote the 'preacher'? "Better is a dinner of herbs where love is, than a stalled ox and hatred". I laugh. What the hell could I do with a stalled ox except use the manure for the garden? And, living alone, have no one to love or hate except self. Am my own best friend anyway. Neighbours came back unexpectedly this afternoon owing to bad weather at holiday resort.

5 June 1987

Dull rather cool morning. Forecast of more rain. 60 degrees in shop. Cloudy most of day. Rain arrived late afternoon and continued until after nightfall, heavy and prolonged. I take the "Guardian". Somewhat highbrow in places. There has been some controversy lately about the difference between poetry and prose. One man, a Mr Dunne, solved the problem with the following:

> There was a young fellow named Fauls
> Walked into the sea up to his knees.

That is prose. If he had gone in a little further it would have been poetry. Illuminating ain't it? So, all you uncultured people who read this at some future date — you now know the difference between poetry and prose.

15 June 1987

Arose early to receive a consignment of coal etc. Have large enough stock of solid fuel to last well into next Winter, or alternatively until I reach that state where peace and tranquility are both unbroken and eternal. Had light breakfast. Journey down village to collect pension and pay for papers. Left instructions to change delivery of "Guardian" to "Independent". "Guardian" now becoming too right wing. In Post Office picked up pamphlet about 'Music at Ratlinghope'. This stirred memories. The Ratlinghope that I remember was a secluded wooded valley. Time 1930s. One old church, one old cottage (no doubt in bygone days home to the church incumbent) and a churchyard. The cottage at that time was occupied by a middle aged lady of no common origin. If not out of the top drawer, at least out of the second. A lonely place to live. I had been sent there with another man to clear the chimney of jackdaws' nests. We cleared away three barrow loads of twigs and rubbish and, even as we worked, jackdaws arrived with further twigs to drop down chimney. I asked the lady if she had any fear of living alone there. She said "No, I have two dogs and a double barrelled shotgun" — and seemed capable of using it. Also, if spirits roamed the churchyard at night they were more to be pitied than feared. I agreed and thought, as the Duke of Wellington remarked on a quite different occasion, "It makes one proud to be English." But that was a long time ago.

12 noon — still wet and dark. Listened to "Poetry Please" on radio. One item asked for and read was "Bingham on the Rhine". My mother often recited it to me as a child. She was very patriotic and fully believed in that old lie "Dulce et decorum est pro patria mori". So no doubt did I until I came to the Somme and Paschendale and discovered that it is one thing to get all starry eyed and romantic about a sword hanging on "the cottage walls of Bingham" and another to take that same sword and stick it in the gut of a young man just out of his boyhood or some mother's son or girl's lover or child's father; or to lob a couple of Mill's bombs into a dugout or wrecked house or trench and listen to the scream that follows, without pity or remorse. To argue that in a different case this could have happened to you is neither here nor there, rather a condemnation of the evil men who cause war in order to further their lust for

power, or greed for wealth. And so it goes on, as ever. The wicked flourish and the innocent suffer. But enough of the past. Had a mind to decorate the back porch but, owing to the damp weather and the hosing down I gave it yesterday, put if off until sunshine dries it. Did however wash the curtains. Still on clothes line and no doubt still wet. I await events. What will come, will come.

24 June 1987

Cool and cloudy at first. Warm with sunshine after midday. Arose in reasonable time. Travelled to Shrewsbury on 11.25am bus. Lady (youngish) who boarded the bus in front of me wore a tight pair of much washed jeans and had a bottom the size of a hot air balloon. Husband would have to get out of bed when she wished to turn over. But everything has its compensations. During Winter months, a well padded wife is better than central heating. Met Julia and girls in Shrewsbury. Returned on same bus as self and remained for refreshments until time for girls to attend dancing classes. Later FW called with Jehovah's Witness mags. Day remains fine and dry. Bought some 'chitterlings' in Market Hall. Many years since last enjoyed them. Cook them for evening meal.

29 June 1987

Very warm. 75 degrees in shop. 80 by midday. Did necessary chores and shopping. Got form from Post Office to redeem Premium Bonds. Useless investment so far. Completed and posted same. Listened "Poetry Please" on radio. One item requested was Tennyson's "Come into the Garden Maud". Well, the sophisticated Maud of a romantic bygone age with flowing tresses and long dress is one thing, the modern Maud in tight jeans and expensive hair-do is another. She would reply "No soap, Buster. I know why you want to go into the garden. I've heard it all before". Well, times change. Hope to do a little weeding as afternoon cools.

Did so, but soon tired.

13 August 1987

Much warmer and humid. 62 degrees in shop. Reached 72 or over later. Usual chores. Win came out. Cooked excellent lunch. Relieved me of that chore. Warm all day. No doubt cold again tomorrow. Climate topsy turvey. I am sensitive to the changing temperature. Do not adapt as in past years. No doubt age asserting itself. To sum up:

Down the swift tide of life I am gliding,
Days of my childhood are left far behind.
Oft in my memory rises a picture,
Calling things joyful or sad to the mind;
When of a morning I welcome the sunrise
Or bid it goodbye as it sets in the west,
I think of the days when I rose up before it
And the hours were joyful with no thought of rest.

14 August 1987

Rather cold again. 60 degrees in shop. Below 70 all day. Usual chores. Sat for a while in back porch. Turned rather cold, so came indoors. Made fire in Parkray once more. Became more comfortable. Made midday meal of odds and ends. Listened for a while to talk on radio about saints. Never had much use for saints myself. At best, their goodness is purely negative. My mother would have described them as a chip in the milk pan — if anyone alive today knows what a milk pan is or was. For myself, I would say it were better far to ease one breast of grief or wipe the tear from one small eye, then sit and mourn the sorrows of the world in musty churches with priests paid to pray. The people who run Oxfam, Save the Children Fund and such like are a lot nearer the gates of the Kingdom of Heaven than all the religious organisations thought of.

6 September 1987

Rather cold morning and low cloud. No rain as of yet. 59 degrees in shop. Cool outdoors. Made fire in Parkray and ate my meagre breakfast in its comforting warmth. Little to do by way of household chores except iron a few shirts etc from yesterday's wash. Afraid I am reaching the statge of senility, decrepitude, old age — call it what you will — when one wishes to sit alone and dream. Dream of what? The past. Well the past had its moments as well as its hardships. No doubt I was fortunate in that I expected little of life. All I expected, like any commoner born in the 19th century, and all I was taught to expect was hardship and ill treatment — and that is mostly what I received. If I appear unduly pessimistic, I am not, I simply state facts. There have been times of extreme joy and happiness to balance the picture, such as being accepted in marriage by the girl of one's choice, the birth of one's first child and the meeting again of old comrades after years of parting. Such things give lasting joy and pleasant memories. Dream of the present? Ever with us and transient as thoughts.

Now midday. Sunday 6th September 1987. Rain, forecast earlier, pattering down on the roof of the back porch where I write this and the few moments I spent writing it have now slipped away into eternity and perhaps oblivion. Who knows? Where am I? Oh dreams. Only the future left to dream about and that is in the hands of the Eternal. Why disquiet oneself for naught? Be concerned with trivial things only. Says the poet "Trifles make the sum of life". Today "Gardener's Question Time" returns to the radio, also "Down Your Way" — new series — at 5pm. Both favourites of mine.

Later. Dreams did not last long. After dinner J&S, listened 'GQT'. A short nap then prepared another box of plums for freezer. Rain now mostly cleared. Short bursts of sunshine, so went for lengthy walk along Leigh Road. Met no-one. Returned 5pm. New series of "Down Your Way" of no interest. Tea of wholemeal bread and butter and mixed fruit, then the first episode of "Vanity Fair". Very good. Worth following.

27 September 1987

Awoke to a dry cold morning. 50 degrees in shop. Rather cold out-

Wedding Day 4th November 1922

doors. Felt fresh and very much alive, owing perhaps to the bracing air. Ironed yesterday's wash and did general household chores. Later took enjoyable walk as far as Plox Green. Called in at the Pottery, but no small jugs on display. On outward journey two cars, at different times, pulled up alongside. One enquired the way to Snailbeach, the other to Leominster (I mean the occupants enquired not the car). I have no doubt, like Balaam's ass, a speaking car will arrive sometime or other, perhaps with greater intelligence than some of the drivers. Walked back through the Council estate. Wind by now cold and turning northerly. Built fire in front room and had a solitary tea by its relaxing warmth.

3 October 1987

Warmer. 56 degrees in shop. Heavy mist. Soon cleared. Sun shone. Did weekly wash, also dried and ironed. Watched racing from Newmarket and Chepstow. Bathed and changed. Was replacing slippers with shoes when something drew my attention. Later, half way down village for a carton of fruit juice, discovered I had on one shoe and one slipper. Did not turn back, affected a limp in case anyone remarked on it. No one did. Had bad pain in right hip as a result. Much better tonight. Home from evening out 11.20pm. Beer up in price 4p per pint.

8 October 1987

Cold with wet, blustery winds. 50 degrees in shop. Reports of gales and heavy rain on south coast and in north west. Could do little but keep home tidy and prepare simple meals, then sit and dream and doze and read "Independent". Half gale outside. Changed library books. One book I selected has paranormal or supernatural stories. Admittedly fiction or near-fiction. Well, truth is said to be stranger than fiction as many of us, including myself, know. I can here relate two out of several incidents which have happened to me. In the early 1920s I was returning home late on Sunday night in Winter from an evening spent with my future wife, pushing my cycle up a road on a hillside. As I did so, I saw coming towards me, or rather to meet me, what I thought to be someone carrying an old fashioned candle-lit horn lantern. When it was opposite me, I saw to my great surprise that the lantern was travelling of its own volition or carried by an invisible figure. It passed on. Mystified, I stopped — fear being then, as now, an unknown quality. I placed my cycle on the roadside and started in pursuit. In vain. When I stopped, the light stopped but moved when I did. I abandoned the search. The experience was never repeated, though I travelled the route many times afterwards. We were married the following November. No one I related it to had heard about the light. Indeed I was mostly disbelieved. The other uncanny experience took place about the same period of time. On the road between Shelve and Pennerley there was at that time a gate in a boundary fence across the road, in a hollow called White Way Dale. Twice, cycling there around midnight, this gate opened for me of its own accord and closed when I had passed. I inspected the gate later during daylight hours and the spring catch was in perfect condition. I have had other experiences of a similar nature. I would here impress upon the reader of this (if such there ever be) — do not be afraid of the paranormal. If the spirits or life-force (call them what you will) wish to get in touch with you, they either want to help you or need help themselves. There are more facets to the invisible world than we know of. I am quite serious about this.

1 November 1987

Complete change in weather today. November breaks with a calm clear morning. A pale Autumn sun shines faintly upon our northern world as if to say "Be at peace and rest, within a few short months I will be back to warm you, as I now go to warm your southern neighbours". The fog of recent days has departed, we hope for a lengthy period. A few fleecy white clouds float, almost static against the blue orb of the heavens. In our little corner of the world for one short moment in the ocean of time, all is tranquility and peace. So good in fact that I sit for a time in the back porch and dream of former happier days, until reality forces itself once more upon me. I complete my Sunday morn chores. I did ask the newsagent to deliver the "Observer" for the Winter months. It has not arrived. An oversight no doubt. Little matter, tomorrow it will be forgotten. Time, like an everflowing stream, will have bourne all thought of it away into the ocean of eternity. After lunch — supplied by my good neighbour — rested a while. Come 2pm listened to "Gardener's Question Time". Later potted some tulip bulbs for early display next Spring (or so I hope). Later, a walk up Callow Road. Reached Bank Farm this time. Only other person out was a man travelling at twice my rate of walking. By then, daylight was failing and evening mists had started to envelope the landscape and obscure the distant hills. Quiet and serenity reigned. Apart from the glimmer of lights in the village below, one could imagine oneself alone with nature.

Evening passed rapidly with radio, TV and good book. Tomorrow is another day and another week.

3 November 1987

Still cold outdoors with persistent fog obscuring hills. 50 degrees in shop. Not a pleasant day to be about. "Meals on wheels" comes back today after midterm break. Price of dinner has risen two pence. Fog thickened during afternoon. Decided I needed exercise and change, so donned anorak and gloves and ventured out. Owing to cold, turned back before reaching target.

So, poor old Bill went for a walk
But had to turn back early;
The fog affects his heart and lungs
And makes him rather surly.
So — it's no go for a walk today,
It's no go for the frisky;
All I need is an easy chair
And a bottle of Irish whiskey.

Back home found the chair, also two fingers of Scotch with hot water and sugar and soon recovered. Have in mind a visit to Shrewsbury tomorrow

10 November 1987

Early low cloud and a clammy damp mist surrounds all things. 47 degrees in shop. Some rain during night. Usual household chores. Enjoyable and tasty meal from "meals on wheels" at lunchtime. About 2pm the weather cleared and a weak Autumn sun enlivened my heart and mind. Made the most of the opportunity to finish off the compost heap and cover it from rain and frost, trusting with the help of Mother Nature to obtain therefrom, at some future date, food and sustenance for my vegetable garden. It is wise to return all waste to that great cubical (or is it cubicle?) of nature — Mother Earth. For they who feed the earth benefit mankind. In return she will give us, like milk from a mother's breast, food for both seedlings and mature plants. I also gave a protective covering of peat or other available material to the roots of any none too hardy flowering shrubs. It was enjoyable to get outdoors for a change and to do this under a clear Autumn sky in the cool but cold outdoors, with the rich smells of the earth pervading all things. Evening light lasted until 5pm, by which time my ageing body cried "enough". Alas, storms forecast for tomorrow.

27 November 1987

First real frost of this season. 39 degrees in shop. Ice on soft water tub. Not welcome. Afternoon with J&S to funeral service of distant cousin's widow at More. A really beautiful old church with box pews (oak and carved). Attended service there regularly when I resided in the parish, after First World War finished. Took communion. Had a dream, alas to be shattered like many others. Church and surroundings very much as then, but now lit by electricity. Sixty seven years gone by and my contemporaries lie in the dust of the earth. "And many of those that sleep in the dust of the earth shall awake". So be it.

9 December 1987

Very cold again. 35 degrees in shop. Fairly hard frost outdoors. Cold and clear air most of day. Temp in shop remained under 40. Stayed around home for warmth and comfort most of time. During afternoon attended funeral service of good friend and one-time domino and drinking partner FR. Service at village and buried in churchyard in same grave, I presume, as his late wife. Church full to capacity. Felt happy to be able to pay final respects. Had one last look at coffin in the ground. Whispered 'So long Fred. Next time we enjoy drink and dominoes together will be in the Kingdom of Heaven — always assuming that we both make it and that they have D and D there'. And why not? JC said He would drink new wine there with His followers. Card and short note from Alberta, USA in post. Said she was slowly recovering from eye operation.

6 January 1988

Like the 'Sentinel in Whitehall Gate', who at the time of the Great Armada "looked forth into the night", I arose from slumber sometime before 9am this morning and looked forth. Not on a streak of blood and light, but on a cold wet windy morn with signs of snow on Stiperstones.

Undecided if to dress or not, but love of comfort prevailed and, after a brief prayer of thanksgiving to the Eternal for a warm and comfortable home and a well fed body, crept back into bed. Next period of consciousness started 10.15. Felt no shame.

Usual household chores. Weather very unpleasant, so stayed about home. Had such a large number of electric heaters that advertised one (convector) in local shop. Couple phoned and later called and purchased it. Stayed up until nearly 1am watching a serio-comic film about First World War 1914-1918. At once hilarious and sad. Poured scorn on people who command. One thing wrong. It showed poppies growing on the battle field. There were none. The only living things — animate or inanimate — that existed on the battlefields of Flanders, apart that is from suffering humanity, were lice who thrived on the living and maggots and rats as large as rabbits that thrived on the flesh of the unburied dead. And I should know. But that was a long time ago.

29 January 1988

Cold clear morning. Pleasant after yesterday's clouds and damp air. 40 degrees in shop. Afternoon especially fine and dry, enhances life — and we start February two days hence. AP and wife came with "meals on wheels". He remarked how well I looked and young. I replied that perhaps I was in my second childhood, but with afterthought said that could not be. As Ronnie Barker once remarked, "I went straight from the cradle into slavery". Well, if not quite so bad as that, I must have been old when I was born, and a loner. Sometime, if granted life and continued intelligence by the Eternal, I would like to write an account of my early life. Especially poignant perhaps would be about acting as a child bearer to children who died early, often before school age. I am one who survived, more by the grace of the Eternal than anything else. My only brother did not. Now 5pm. Evening darkens, but a completely dry day and barometer falling. Interest account from Building Society in post. Jim called by for tea. Storm warnings all around coast.

12 February 1988

Bright sunshine but very cold wind. 43 degrees in shop with radiator on. Too cold for any outdoor activity. So, after light brek, retired to Summer's day warmth of Summer House. First edition of new-look "Guardian" out today. Paper and print an improvement. I shall no doubt have many idle or part-idle hours and days until the sun warms the Earth once more and the resurrection of plant life brings joy again to the northern hemisphere. I am happy, though perhaps without joy, to anticipate life's return. I am glad O Earth my mother to be still full of pulsating life in the midst of this awakening, like a boat upon a flooded river which strives and sings from pure ecstasy. And it is still given to me to be a man. But to return to more mundane things. The sun is fast westering; shedding its life-giving rays on other parts of the Earth, to return to us — or so we hope — on the morrow. I have still a few duties indoor. Jim called by for tea.

Later the phone rang. When I picked it up, a voice gave an address. Said they were fitted kitchen experts. "Would I care to consult them?" I thanked them for calling but said "No, my cook is well satisfied with kitchen as at present." As I live alone and am cook and general dogsbody to self, this was quite correct.

16 March 1988

Somewhat drier day. Short periods of rain. 50 degrees in shop. Clear dry intervals, though without sunshine. Slept very late but no matter. All went according to plan, or rather no plan. Just drifted. One journey down village for supplies. Purchased seven small Easter cards for relatives in USA. Keep in touch. Postage will cost more than cards. Write them tonight, post next week. Poverty diet all day, so cooked excellent evening meal — sausage, egg, bacon and fried potatoes followed by stewed plums (from freezer) and cream. Gave thanks to the Eternal for healthy appetite and wherewithall to satisfy same, unlike so many poor creatures (human) in this sad world of ours. No doubt most of this is caused by human greed, but such it is. King David of the Israelites of old is reported to have said that he had never seen the righteous foresaken or his seed beg bread. No doubt in many ways a brave and good man but mistaken, at least in today's history. I have seen the children of good people beg for food, to the shame of us all.

10 May 1988

A very warm morning with sunshine all day. 58 in shop. Reached 70s later. Really a day for joy and happiness. This is the ninety second anniversary of my birth. Feel old and decrepit after very bad night with chest pains. No doubt stomach trouble. Must be more careful with food intake. But such things hit one's ego and self confidence. I say to myself "How much better it is that a man should die in battle in the glory of youth when his blood is hot, than live to a miserable old age and die in bed" (which, in my case, may God forbid). Then a voice from the past echoes down the tunnel of time saying "You are selfish. You consider only your own feelings. What about your parents who would have grieved for you after the death of your brother? What about your wife with whom you spent fifty seven happy years? What about your children and their children who would never have been born?" It is better to forget self and leave one's fate in the hands of the Eternal, who knows the beginning and the end. Received many cards and greetings from well wishers. Spent most of day basking in sunshine in back porch. Fasted all day. Retired to bed 9.30pm with drink made from egg beaten up in milk.

15 May 1988

Very warm with much sunshine. 62 degrees in shop. Promise of fair weekend. Live mostly outdoors now, so little housework. Ironed yesterday's wash. Spent remaining morning hours reading "Observer". Afternoon, following dinner J&S and "Gardener's Question Time", potted some more Summer-flowering plants to go out when Summer does arrive. Later took walk up Callow Road. Perhaps because of heat, it seemed more tiring than usual. Nevertheless the walk was a delight. Stretches of broom blossom, golden and shining in random profusion, and other multi-coloured wayside flowers. Met several other people out, also enjoying the fine day, including K who walked with me awhile but turned back across road to quarry. Returned home shortly before 6pm to enjoy very welcome pot of tea. Later listened and watched "Highway" with Harry Secombe from Brecon and Brecon Beacons. He sang, amongst others, the Battle Hymn of the Republic — "Mine Eyes Have Seen the Glory of the Coming of the Lord." How much more appropriate it would be to have this sung over one's mortifying remains at a funeral service than the usual mournful dirges — and the Trumpet Voluntary instead of a Dead March. "O Death where is your sting?" Becoming increasingly bad at spelling. Have to consult dictionary more often. 8.02pm. Sun now setting behind factory.

2 June 1988

Cloudy and cool at first. Improved before noon. Day became really warm with a few white fleecy clouds drifting aimlessly and leisurely about in the blue dome of the heavens, saying to mortal man "Peace. Why do you rush about as though there were no tomorrow, like ants that have no future but slavery in continuity?" Posted few birthday cards. Called at Post Office for stamps. Queue waiting for counter service. One or two complaining about climate in June. Told them to accept what comes and to thank God it is not worse. Received no comment. Wondered about raspberry crop. Would it be ready before holiday? Sought last year's diary. Found I started picking first week in July. Seem somewhat earlier this year. So no cause to worry. Excellent crop anyway. Shall have a full freezer. Heard today of death of old friend GH.

11 June 1988

Much happier outlook. Sun shines bright and clear in a cloudless sky. Forgotten is the damp and cool of the last three days — and tomorrow is yet to come, bring what it may. No doubt all things are part of the eternal plan. I consume my meagre breakfast of cereal in the warmth and comfort of the back porch and marvel at the wonders of nature and also at the intricacy of the human body. It is written "God made man in His own image". Not so, wrote Hannen Swaffer some years ago in the "People" newspaper, the reverse is the case — man made God in his image. He did not try to explain how man came to exist. And I for one most emphatically refuse to believe that man, with his reasoning powers and thumbs turning inward (not possessed by any other creature on Earth), started life as a small piece of jelly washed up on the shore of some obscure ocean a million or so years ago.

Did a reasonably sized weekly wash which dried perfectly outdoors. With fine days, live as much as possible outdoors and eat cold meals and salad. Life uncertain anyway and at my age the old boy with the scythe could call any time saying "Come on Buster your time is called". To which no doubt I shall reply "Where the BH have you been until now? I have waited a long time". Time is now 12.30. Still warm but with some clouds drifting from easterly direction. Must think about food. Did so. Cloud thickened later, but by then had retired to chair.

12 June 1988

A near perfect morning. Sun shines in an almost cloudless sky. A few white woolly clouds drifting leisurely from an easterly direction. 61 degrees in shop. Barometer slowly rising. Although a near perfect morning, yet something lacking. Vague and indistinct. An emptiness of spirit perhaps. There is always something lacking. No doubt John Bunyan's Pilgrim, when he finally reached the Celestial City and passed through the gates, found it hardly lived up to his fantasies. My idea of Paradise is a place where one could live forever with people one has loved and been loved by in this life and have no thought of tomorrow, for tomorrow there will not be. I would enjoy helping to keep the place tidy and helping others to polish their golden crowns, so long as I was not asked to wear one myself. It would give me a headache. My only head covering is the one Mother Nature gave me. But all this is pure rhetoric. Poof. Wind. Vapourings of a fool. Let us:

> Take the cash and let the credit go,
> Nor heed the rumble of a distant drum!

Afternoon took walk down Plox Green road returning through Council estate. Sun still shines. Met no-one.

Had enjoyable tea of strawberries in syrup from the freezer with ice cream.

3 July 1988

Sunday. A cold unpleasant day. 61 degrees in shop. Cold north east wind and frequent storms. Stayed in bed as long as possible. Did necessary chores. Picked a few raspberries, but was driven indoors by cold and wet. Not a good start for July. Dinner J&S. Listened "Gardener's Question Time". Some interesting items. Come 4pm, started out on walk to exercise and loosen joints. Met three ladies of my acquaintance. Stopped for short conversation. On way home called at Spar stores for cheese-spread for tea. Caught in rain storm before reaching home. Made myself comfortable. 6.40pm good programme on ITV about Salvation Army. Revived memories of long ago. One time, 1914 to be exact, I had a girlfriend in the Salvation Army. Really I was friendly with two sisters — Bessie and Mary Bloomer. They lived with their parents at a house called TE AMU, Boundary Road, Winton, Bournemouth. TE AMU was Maori for "the homeland". Bessie was the one in the SA. She wore the bonnet and cloak and spoke at street meetings. Mary was a Lady's Maid, a kind of dogsbody who did everything for rich women who had money but no sense — secretarial duties, seeing to dress and hair-do etc and no doubt covering for their numerous affairs. I am writing of a bygone age. Mary was tall and elegant, had a rather large nose and was of high intellect and intelligence. We corresponded throughout my sojourn in France and Belgium. She wrote long interesting letters about things in England. 'Cabbages and kings' one might say. It is possible she would have married me had I asked her, but it would not have worked out. With her superiority, she would have despised me after a few years. So I did not and she did not. I hope to renew acquaintance when the Kingdom of Heaven comes to earth. But why, you may ask, all this rigmarole? Well, just retrospective after the TV programme and the reader (if such there ever be) can smile and pass on. If you ever live to old age you also will have dreams.

28 July 1988

Similar to yesterday (stormy with blustery winds) but more sunshine during afternoon. 61 degrees in Summer House. Win came out. Changed library books. Otherwise uneventful day. In post, a card of Oast Houses in Kent from C&F. Also communication from BBC saying a poem I had requested would be read on Monday August 22 on "Poetry Please". Poem 'On Time' by John Milton. I am a glutton for poetry and have a small library of poetry books. My favourites, if any, being Burns, Milton, Tennyson and Byron more or less in that order. I also have a great affection for Wilfred Owen, killed just before the Great War finished. A sad loss to England and humanity in general. Unfortunately a great many people do not share my love of poetry and make an excuse to leave when I discourse on it. To me, poetry is the yeast that lightens the dough of civilisation and brings romance to the souls of men. If poets sometimes do call an armistice with truth, it is all in the interests of goodwill.

26 September 1988

Warm and dull. Some bursts of sunshine. 60 degrees in Summer House. Somewhat normal Autumn day (here must record Mrs E Davies just brought me two small fruit pies. Home baked. Gave her some raspberries from my freezer). Arose rather late this morning. No matter, nothing lost. Had dish of porridge for breakfast, which was a mistake as my stomach cannot assimilate during early part of day. Must keep to tea, biscuits or slice of toast. I never learn. Usual Monday chores. Paid for papers and collected pension from Post Office. Although not rich, I am comfortably situated as regards money. I would have wished my parents in their old days to have been so comfortably placed. I have an interesting book from the library "Mare's Milk and Wild Honey — A Shropshire boyhood." Time about 1939. I could write an equally interesting book about my boyhood which was nearly fifty years earlier. On second thoughts, I will leave it to my grandson Peter who is a sound literary man. I would entitle my book "Hasty Pudding and Kettle Broth" — some of the food we filled our empty stomachs with in those days. I was born in 1896 on a small hill farm among the Shropshire hills, one of a family of five — three sisters older and one brother younger. He died young. I will not weary the reader with our names. Though never short of food, we were often short of money. Besides scratching some sort of living from the land, my father worked intermittently at local mines — not always in production earning perhaps 15 shillings (75p) per week. So the reader can understand that our young and hungry bellies enjoyed any food that was available. Hasty Pudding was made hanging a pot of skimmed milk over the fire and mixing into it a cupful or so of plain flour (often home grown) and a little salt. Nourishing and filling. But I hardly imagine today's children giving it a welcome as we did. Kettle Broth was also a filling meal. Here we had bread broken into a basin, a few chopped chives, a lump of bacon fat or beef dripping (both plentiful in those days) and hot water poured over the lot. Kettle Broth. Well, sneer if you may, but still better than the diet of the workhouse where so many of my parent's generation ended their pitiful lives. My mother was a wonderful woman. How she struggled to keep us fed and clothed is beyond my comprehension and not always appreciated, by me at any rate at that time. Only by hindsight. We often had bread and milk with a cupful of pinhead oatmeal tipped into the pot of milk. I hated it because the oatmeal was gritty and no doubt regularly complained. My mother would often get annoyed (undoubtedly with good cause), also my school teacher and others, beause I questioned everything. I was always asking Why? Why? Why? I was told on innumerable occasions — nearly daily — by my mother and others "I pity the woman who ever marries you". It was only in later years and with hindsight that I discovered how right they were and how my wife (surely the best ever) suffered with me for fifty seven years. No matter. Come the Resurrection we will all have a good laugh about it, or so I believe. Well, enough of that I hope for Peter Francis to start his book "Hasty Pudding and Kettle Broth". I give it my blessing. May it be as popular as Peter Davies' "Mare's Milk and Wild Honey" and may the blessing of the Eternal rest on all who read it. It is true in substance but only half, or perhaps less than half, of the complete truth. By then I shall have gone on the journey which man only travels once and come face to face with Him who made the universe and all the angels of God who hasten to do His will.

7 October 1988

Very cold, wet, windy morning after stormy night. Spent early part of day indoors. Made open fire in front room to combat cold. Very cosy. Jim called for tea. Letter from C&F in post. Also, sometime during day, card pushed through letter box saying Congregational minister called but I was not at home. Wrote and posted a short note to him, thanking him for calling and regretting I was not at home. Pure politeness. Have no further use for organised religion anyway. It is all ritual and dogma, dressing in funny clothes and carrying candles and things about. It is my hope one day to meet Him who made and saved the world and ask His views. I have no doubt they will be more of pity than condemnation. Cold and dry evening.

21 October 1988

Another fine day with much sunshine. 55 degrees in Summer House. Winter sunshine only reaches there for short time each day now. Will have to desert it, except for plants and cleaning, until next April. Household chores and odds and ends. Mid afternoon, was about to get bath and change when front door bell rang. Congregational minister who left card short time ago. Invited him in. Gave light refreshments. Had animated conversation of many things. Mainly poetry and religion.

23 October 1988

Summer time finished indeed. Dark and dreary. 57 in Summer House. Thick fog. A few household chores. Ironed yesterday's wash. Dinner

J&S. Listened "Gardener's Question Time". Later, hazy Autumn sunshine broke through a cloudy sky. Air mild and pleasant. Decided to take long walk and enjoy what could be the dregs of the old or the opening of a new period of life's joys.

> For in life's road, though thorns abundant grow,
> There still are joys that some will never know —
> Joys which the dead companions of my prime
> Missed as they sank into the stream of time.
>
> Oh though who bid'st the vernal juices rise,
> Thou on whose blast Autumnal foliage flies,
> Let peace ne'er leave me nor my heart grow cold
> Whilst life and sanity are mind to hold.

Walked the Leigh road so far as Etsell cottage. Still fresh and vigorous. Tossed a coin — should I carry on to Drury Lane and Plox Green or turn back? Came down tails, so turned back. Met only one other person out, a lady walking a dog. Exchanged greetings.

Darkness fell at 5.30 and still two months until shortest day. Settled in front room with books and TV and fire in grate.

12 December 1988

Dull and mild. 50 degrees in Summer House. Felt really unwell. Struggled along as best I could. Breakfast — cup of tea and one biscuit. Made way down village to pay for papers and collect pension. Post consisted of Christmas card from niece Alberta, USA and interesting postcard from F, with picture of an old wheelwright repairing a farm cart wheel. Memories. When I was a child (if I ever was a child, which I doubt) my over-riding ambition was to be a wheelwright and joiner. Would lie awake at night making schemes and plans. Alas, vain hope. Parents too poverty stricken to think of apprenticeship, which then carried no pay. Spent four useless years until 18 in no-end jobs. Then got caught up for five years (which should have been the best of my life) exterminating — or risking being exterminated by — the flower of the young manhood of Europe. No-one will read this until I am dead, but when on the final day I stand naked before the throne of eternal justice (as all men must) what do I answer? When a risen person points at me and says "I am the enemy you killed, my friend. But for you I could have had the love of a good woman and nursed our children on my knee. But I had none of these things. You did" — where lies the fault?

Afternoon posted cards (airmail) to USA. FW called about lunchtime with Jehovah's Witness mags. Had cup of coffee together and talk. Health improved during afternoon. On way home from farm with eggs, called at local shop. Purchased bottle of Harvey's Bristol Cream Sherry in hopes of pepping my old body up a little.

16 December 1988

Temp still 50 degrees in Summer House. Air cleared later. Became cool. Some bursts of Wintery sunshine. Body in poor condition today. Fed on liquid nourishment. Put "meals on wheels" in fridge until tomorrow. Hoping for the best. Big upset in Tory politics today. John Biffen, member for Oswestry, states that we should abandon nuclear weapons (he has already had the push). Also, Edwina Curry castigates poultry farmers for producing unfit food. She will no doubt have to resign or be pushed (she has). I would strongly advise both of them to come over and join us. Have their names placed among the Socialist immortals. I have been a Socialist from the night I was conceived (always supposing it was night) although my mother was a true blue Tory. In spite of holding staunch Christian beliefs, she had belonged to the Primrose League — as I discovered from her papers after she died. I must have been an irritation to her even in the womb. I certainly was afterwards. May the Eternal bless her memory. I do. She lived a hard and exacting life.

2 January 1989

Awoke to a dull colder day. Temp below 45 degrees in Summer House. Condition rather better at first. Slipped back later, perhaps because of cold air. Breakfasted on tea and slice of toast. After midday, Brian brought me a plateful of 'chicken and chips'. Ate and enjoyed most of it. Late afternoon, Mrs J brought me a dish of trifle. Ate half for tea. Other half in fridge for tomorrow. Everyone good and helpful. Film on BBC1 tonight — Mary Webb's 'Precious Bane'. Copied from one of her rather sad books. Well, I suppose one half of our lives is tragic. Take note of recent events in Europe alone. Perhaps remarks on film tomorrow.

Stayed up until 11.30 plus to watch film. Much impressed. Period some forty or fifty years even before my time and I was born in 1896. But lived in film and lived it again after retiring to my bed. Two things only out of place. The man mowing corn and the cross cut saw. I was reared (if that is the right phrase) on a small hill farm and by the age of fourteen or so must have mown, or helped to mow, many acres of ripe corn. Holding the scythe in a half stooping position, one laid out the swathe symmetrically — heads of corn lying perfectly in same direction — ready for tying up (an art in itself). As for the saw with its bunches of three teeth, I do not call to mind this type in general use before the 1920s. No matter, a touching and moving film.

10 January 1989

Hurrah! January in double figures. Daylight until 5pm. In fact could see to get about until 5.30. Weather cooler. 45 degrees in Summer House. Windows misted over last night. Still, warm for January. Welcomed by me without a doubt. The earth continues its eternal (?) orbital passage around the sun, in spite of the ineptitude of man. I write "eternal" here with a question mark. Who am I to see into the distant future? I have crocuses in bloom in the garden. Even a blossom or two on Japonica. Hellebore still a brave show. Had a rather bad start today. Better later. Accepted "meals on wheels" and ate most of it and all the sweet. Bulk of week's wash now packed safely away. I took one or two articles to iron. Some rain forecast for tomorrow.

Here illness overtook me. Had to call in doctor. Recommended hospital. Ambulance called about 6pm. Copthorne South, ward 9.

With wife Adeline and children John, Jim and Winnie

Three weeks. Only hazy recollection. Since then — nights with J&S, days at home. Memory uncertain. Future uncertain and in the hands of the Eternal. Who am I? Quote from Scriptures "I will have mercy on whom I will have mercy". So be it. Leave space for possible future notes.

9 March 1989
Try to pick up threads of life. Day dull and very windy. 42 degrees in Summer House. Local landscape and gardens show signs of early Spring. Daffs, narcissi and tulips a defiant and life heartening show. Win comes out weekly now. With J's help, changed library books. Daylight much extended. One would hope and pray for lots of life-giving sunshine. Wish! May I have daily strength to continue "Diary" and also regain a sense of humour.

15 March 1989
Much better day. Long periods of sunshine. Health very poorly. Doctor called and prescribed change of tablets. K called for short time also FW with mag. Later Julia and Angela. Gave them light refreshments.

My Grandfather died on April 7th 1989, just five weeks before his 93rd birthday. His final diary entry, dated **16 March**, reads:

A dull rather mild day. Average 50 degrees indoors. No sunshine. Win came out. Cooked good midday meal. Left two more in freezer. RL called. Brought some eating apples. Gave him liquid refreshment. He said lots of people down village inquiring about me. Nice to think so.

The only memorial my Grandfather would have wished for was to be remembered as "a true son of the Stiperstones."